Economic Development Marketing

PRESENT AND FUTURE

Anatalio C. Ubalde
& Eric Simundza

For more information, vist:

GIS Planning: www.GISplanning.com

ZoomProspector: www.ZoomProspector.com

UC Berkeley: www.berkeley.edu

ISBN: 978-0-615-25146-2

Printed in the United States of America

Table of Contents

Introduction

"It is not the strongest of the species that survives, nor the most intelligent that survives. It is the one that is the most adaptable to change."

– Charles Darwin

INTRODUCTION

Inertia is a powerful force that is impeding the effectiveness of the economic development profession. Economic developers are implementing specific marketing strategies because it's what they've been doing in the past, it's what their elected officials understand because that's how the organization has always done it, they've gotten awards for what they did in the past, and because it feels safe – even if it doesn't work at all.

There are many ways that communities have been marketed. Some of the marketing tactics that have historically worked continue to work but many are not effective anymore.

Few people in the economic development profession graduate with a college degree in economic development. Instead, much of the professional education comes on-the-job and by attending conferences or professional development trainings. A problem with the economic development marketing training courses is that many of the introductory classes should be titled "A History of Economic Development Marketing" but they are called "An Introduction to Economic Development Marketing." So the people attending the classes are confused because they think they are getting an introduction when they are actually getting a history. And it's a history of many economic development marketing strategies that worked in the past but don't work well anymore. Unfortunately, some of those attending leave thinking that all marketing strategies are equal when they really aren't.

Economic development marketing is evolving. I saw these changes in communication, technology and new media unfolding when I worked in local economic development. The transformation became clearer to me as I moved to the private sector to start GIS Planning and worked across North America serving hundreds of communities, from the largest cities, states and utility companies to the many small and medium sized communities.

One of my frustrations related to talking about the changes in marketing places was that there were limited data with which to measure these changes. Sometimes at national conferences when experts within our profession would quote percentages and statistics, I would ask them for their information sources and they would tell me "Oh, I think it's about that much." Unfortunately for the people that heard their speeches and were going to take action based on them, they thought those numbers were objectively quantified.

There was very little existing national research that was trustworthy or reliable. One of the few exceptions to this was the interesting research by DCI that surveyed businesses and site selectors. However their research didn't go deep enough into understanding the behavior and programs "on the ground" in economic development organizations across the USA that practice marketing.

So I developed a partnership with the University of California at Berkeley to design and implement a national survey about economic development marketing, and then to analyze the results. Two surveys were created. The first was given to economic development practitioners. The second was given to corporate real estate professionals and site selection consultants responsible for making or influencing corporate site location decisions. We would have liked to also have a national survey of businesses of a variety of employment sizes, industry types, and revenue amounts but unfortunately the scope of that project was cost prohibitive. We hope to do something like that next time.

An important reason to do research is that you want to be surprised, and we were definitely surprised by the responses. The results are contained in this book and I won't summarize them in this introduction except to say our profession has plenty of room to improve, we actually know what marketing we should be doing but aren't doing it, and making changes toward more effective strategies will give organizations a meaningful competitive advantage.

Another reason we pursued this survey is because GIS Planning needs to deeply understand the changes happening in the economic development profession so we can continue to stay ahead of the trends, anticipate changes, and develop new ways to make our clients the most successful in effective economic development.

Perhaps the most important reason for this survey is that as economic developers we need to get better. Many, if not most, of the economic development organizations in the USA are publicly funded through taxes on the businesses and residents of the community. We must be good stewards of these public resources and not waste people's money on marketing that doesn't produce results. Also, the work we do is important. We may not save lives like an emergency room doctor but we have the opportunity to improve lives.

I learned very early on while working in local economic development that it was an amazing feeling when someone came up to me to thank me for helping a business open in my city because it gave them a better job. And to the readers of this book, since I imagine it's mostly economic developers reading this, my story is your story and the story of every economic developer who has been thanked by someone who got a new job, a better job, or a path to better employment because of the work you did in your office. Jobs enable so many things in people's lives ranging from paying the mortgage to creating the self-esteem that results from having a job. Although businesses create jobs, economic developers can help foster their success.

So read this book and then let's get to work. We have people to help, so let's not waste any time, money or marketing.

Anatalio C. Ubalde

San Francisco, California

Summary

SUMMARY

Economic developers must be adept at implementing marketing strategies to promote their communities and grow their local economies. They must know how to communicate with businesses to be successful in this pursuit. Recent changes in communication, especially the rise of the Internet, are profoundly altering how business communication and research takes place, and are influencing how businesses engage in the process of site selection and interact with economic development organizations.

Many economic development agencies are responding to these changes through the way they market their communities and provide their services.[1] Others have been left scrambling to make sense of how their industry is changing. Economic development organizations and local governments often do not match the speed of the private sector when it comes to restructuring business practices to respond to new challenges and opportunities. At the same time, benchmarking the success of economic development marketing efforts is difficult, as there are no typical "sales" data to point to as is the case with typical marketing.

There is limited long-term research about economic development marketing strategies' efficacy or the different ways of measuring success. This is further complicated by the lack of industry-standardized or easily-measurable metrics economic developers use to evaluate their own marketing programs. Technology advances and globalization changes have only increased the dynamic nature of marketing, so economic developers are now reevaluating how to most effectively communicate with businesses. As the paths of communication between communities and business have broadened and the business demands for rapid information communication have increased, the necessity of effective marketing communication has become more crucial.

This book, through analysis of a nationwide survey of economic development practitioners, examines how economic developers are using strategies to market their communities and their services[1]. The book investigates changes in marketing over time and the effectiveness of the strategies used. Results from a separate survey of site selection consultants and corporate real estate professionals were brought in to determine how the marketing practices of economic development practitioners compare to the behavior and preferences of those involved in corporate site selection.

This study has resulted in several key findings:

- Economic development organizations' budget allocations for marketing strategies do not always correlate with the effectiveness of each strategy. This indicates a lag between awareness and action. For example, print advertising, which received very low effectiveness ratings, receives the second highest average budget allocation.

- The most effective marketing strategy for economic development is the organization's website. This was consistently reported by both economic developers and site selectors. Face-to-face marketing strategies also received high marks.

- The website was reported by site selectors to be the first point of contact with an economic development organization during the site selection decision making process, rather than personal interaction with staff. 98% of site selectors visit websites of economic development organizations during the process of site selection.

- The majority of economic development organizations are marketing to a national or global audience of businesses.

- Lead generation is the top measure of marketing success for organizations, and the amount of jobs created is the top measure of success for organizations overall. However, manufacturing is the top industry target for economic developers even though it is a declining employment industry. High-growth employment industries such as business services, information, and finance/insurance were all significantly lower priorities for economic developers.

- Large, urban communities targeted industries that create jobs for those in the knowledge economy, such as finance, science, and high-tech. Smaller, rural communities, and to a lesser extent suburban communities, targeted industries that create amenities that attract visitors and provide quality of place for residents, such as retail, accommodation/food service, and arts/entertainment/recreation.

- The industries most targeted by economic development organizations differ from those that are served by corporate real estate professionals and site selectors. Furthermore, the economic development organizations that reported effective marketing results and stronger local economies were those that had campaigns which were aligned more closely with the industry focus of corporate real estate professionals and site selectors.

- Effective marketing was found to be correlated with higher budgets and more staff time devoted to marketing.

- With a few exceptions, the marketing strategies that tend to be outsourced at a high rate also tend to be those strategies that are given low effectiveness ratings.

- Contrary to the larger trend in advertising, economic developers are investing relatively little into online advertising. Spending is scheduled to increase in the next five years.

This book demonstrates which marketing strategies are most and least effective, followed by a discussion of how economic development agencies allocate their budgets among these strategies and for marketing as a whole. It then examines geographic coverage of marketing as well as the industries targeted. At this point, the book pauses to highlight differences in marketing approaches based on organizational structure and characteristics of the communities served. The practices of organizations with effective marketing are then detailed to attain insights as to what leads to success.

The book continues on to highlight patterns in the outsourcing of marketing strategies to help determine the rationale behind the use of consultants. It then discusses the sources of information utilized by corporate real estate professionals during the site selection process. The focus then analyzes economic development websites, including which resources organizations typically provide on their websites and how they are maintained. The book wraps up its discussion of marketing strategies with a look at how organizations benchmark the success of the entire organization and of marketing in particular.

This book can be used by economic development practitioners to better understand the changes in the practice of economic development marketing on a national scale. In the instances where consensus is achieved regarding the merits of particular marketing strategies, this book can serve as a resource on best practices for economic development marketing.

1. Marketing Effectiveness

"We immediately become more effective when we decide to change ourselves rather than asking things to change for us."
— Stephen Covey

1. MARKETING EFFECTIVENESS

There are many different ways to promote a community and the methods are growing in number as new means of communication evolve.[2] Given the choices that economic developers now face, it is important to carefully consider what makes an effective marketing program.

Economic developers were asked to rate the most effective marketing strategies for economic development. The results are shown in Table 1-1. 79% of economic developers rated Internet/website as most effective. The next most highly rated strategies, out-of-town meetings with businesses and site selection consultants/familiarization tours, involve personal contact. The results here indicate that effective marketing must be both high-tech and high-touch, combining effective use of an online presence with personalized, face-to-face service.[3]

Table 1-1. The sixteen most effective marketing strategies used by economic development organizations

Marketing Strategy	Rating Effective[4]
Internet/website	79%
Out-of-town meetings with businesses	72%
Site selection consultants and familiarization tours	64%
Public relations	64%
Special events	56%
E-mail	48%
Targeted lead development databases	43%
Slogans, logo and identity	38%
Trade shows and conferences	36%
Direct mail	26%
Brochures	20%
Print advertising	16%
Videos	14%
Online advertising	13%
TV/radio advertising	10%
Telemarketing	6%

In the separate survey of site selectors, respondents were far more critical in their rating of logo/slogans/identity, as the percent rating this strategy as effective was less than one third of the percent of economic developers rating it effective. Site selectors also gave significantly lower ratings to email, out-of-town meetings with businesses, public relations, and all forms of advertising (print, online, and television/radio).[5] For a complete description, see Table C-1 in the Appendix.

Roughly half of respondents reported that their marketing programs were of average effectiveness (see Figure 1-1) and almost as many believed their marketing programs were effective to very effective. Very few respondents listed their marketing programs as ineffective. It is numerically impossible for a higher percentage to be above average than below, indicating that economic developers may have an unrealistic optimism. This trend was also consistent in the analysis of how economic developers perceived their communities' economic health compared to the rest of the nation (see Figure A-2 in Appendix). However, this phenomenon of groups of people assuming they are typical or above average is not unique to economic development.[6]

Figure 1-1. How economic development organizations rate the effectiveness of their marketing programs and techniques

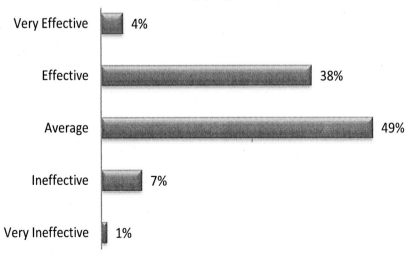

Very Effective — 4%
Effective — 38%
Average — 49%
Ineffective — 7%
Very Ineffective — 1%

2. Budgeting

"My problem lies in reconciling my gross habits with my net income."

— Errol Flynn

2. BUDGETING

No matter how effective a marketing strategy may be, an economic development organization needs an adequately sized budget in order to have an effective marketing program. Each organization must decide how much of its total budget to devote to marketing, as well as how much to devote to each marketing strategy it pursues.

The median marketing budget for respondents was $50,000, while the median budget for the organization as a whole was $500,000, meaning that economic development organizations are typically devoting 10% of their overall budgets for marketing purposes. This percentage tracks with typical figures for public firms across all industries.[7] Organizations that indicated they carry out effective marketing also have larger budgets. For further discussion, please see Section 5, "Practices of Effective Organizations."

Table 2-1. Average budget allocation vs. perceived effectiveness

Marketing Strategy	Average Budget Allocation	Rating Effective
Internet/website	17%	79%
Print advertising	11%	16%
Brochures	11%	20%
Trade shows and conferences	11%	36%
Out-of-town meetings with businesses	10%	72%
Public relations	8%	64%
Special events	7%	56%
Site selection consultants and familiarization tours	6%	64%
Direct mail	5%	26%
E-mail	4%	48%
Slogans, logo and identity	3%	38%
Targeted lead development databases	2%	43%
Videos	2%	14%
TV/radio advertising	1%	10%
Online advertising	1%	13%
Telemarketing	1%	6%

The most effective strategy, Internet/websites, was found to have the highest average budget allocation. However, **budgeting priorities are often not in line with what strategies work**, as seen in Table 2-1. As an example, economic development organizations spend the next highest portion of their budget on print advertising, even though only 16% of organizations rated this as an effective strategy. Brochures and trade shows/conferences ranked 3rd and 4th in terms of budget allotment, but only were perceived as effective by 20% and 36% of respondents, respectively. On the other hand, public relations, special events, and site selection consultants/familiarization tours received comparatively low budget allotments considering their high levels of perceived effectiveness.

Marketing budgets for websites/Internet experienced the largest increases over the past 5 years, and respondents anticipated they would also receive the greatest boost in the years ahead (see Table 2-2). Organizations also put more funding into out-of-town meetings with businesses, which are expected to be funded even more in the next 5 years. Site selection consultants and familiarization tours are also expected to have significantly greater budgeting priority in the next 5 years, while slogans, logo, and graphic identity are expected to have significantly less budgeting allocation in the future. This may mark an attitudinal shift in economic developers away from a focus on branding to a focus on creating virtual and personal relationships, even though economic developers rated branding rather effective, especially compared to the lower value perceptions of site selectors.

The marketing strategies that receive high budget allotments and low effectiveness ratings warrant more scrutiny, and are discussed in more detail in the following sections.

Trade Shows and Conferences

A 2005 study by the Brookings Institution found that even as cities race to construct bigger and better convention centers to take advantage of what had been perceived as a burgeoning market, attendance at the 200 largest trade show events remained at the same level as in 1993. Some cities, including some of the most historically successful convention areas, have experienced declines of over 50% in convention attendance since the late 1990s when attendance was peaking. The authors point out that the decline is not simply due to business shifting from one city to another or the restructuring of certain trade events, but also to "industry consolidation, reductions in business travel in the face of increasing cost and difficulty, and alternative means of conveying and gathering information."[8]

The Internet is undoubtedly one of those alternative means that is undermining the importance of trade events. By recording events and archiving them on websites, marketers can reach more customers with fewer burdens on staff than through traditional trade shows, and the customers are able to control how and when content is viewed. Additionally, web events allow for marketers to easily convert registrants to sales leads.[9]

Print Advertising

National trends in advertising highlight the declining importance of print ads in a media universe that is increasingly positioned online. In an outlook report for 2007 Fitch Ratings wrote: "The trend that will continue to affect the media universe…is the ongoing shift in advertising dollars from traditional media into nontraditional media, most notably the Internet."[10] For example, the Newspaper Association of America forecasted for 2007 that ad spending on the Websites of newspapers would increase 22% from 2006, while at the same time, ad spending in the print editions of those newspapers would increase only 1.2%.[11] The decline in advertising within the site location magazine industry is more moribund and is illustrated in Figure 2-1, which shows ad pages declining in every site location magazine from 1999 to 2007. Ad revenue has also been declining (see Figure C-1 in Appendix). Two of the leading publications for the site location industry have ceased print publication within the past few years: *Plants, Sites & Parks* in 2004 and *Expansion Management* in 2008.

Figure 2-1. Total Annual Ad Pages for Site Location Magazines, 1999-2007

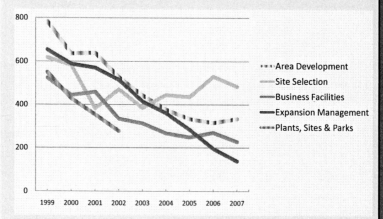

Source: Inquiry Management Systems. No data for PS&P was available in 2003 and 2004.[12]

Over 99% of site location publications are distributed free of charge to business subscribers. As of mid-2007, *Site Selection* was the sole industry publication receiving culation, which amounted to only 0.8% of its total circulation (see Table C-2 in Appendix). Not only are few business customers paying for these publications, but many customers are not even requesting them. As circulation numbers for personal subscription requests have dropped over the years, site location publications have increasingly sent unsolicited subscriptions to executives listed in business directories, such as Dun & Bradstreet.[13] Personal direct requests for the aforementioned site location publications declined from 81% of total circulation at the end of 2000 to 66% in the middle of 2007, while at the same time circulation from business directories grew from 2% to 24% (see Figure C-2 and Table C-3 in Appendix).[14] Excluding *Expansion Management*, the remaining three active print publications send 36% of their magazines to people that have not requested the magazines.

Although the 2008 shuttering of the print version of *Expansion Management* could be assumed to be an opportunity for the remaining publications to absorb its market share, the similar historic evidence does not indicate that will happen. The year after *Plant, Sites & Parks* closed down, its competitors all experienced dramatic drops in the number of advertising pages placed.

Executives in manufacturing industries constituted 69% of the audience for these publications on average in 2007 (see Table C-4 in Appendix). As more manufacturing jobs move out of the United States, site location publications are responding to this trend by running stories about business climates around the world.[15] Local economic development organizations that choose to advertise in these publications are therefore reaching an audience that is primarily made up of businesses in a declining employment sector. Some of these manufacturers are reading the publications to learn more about how they can outsource their labor overseas or implement facility expansion outside of the USA. This situation could present a good marketing opportunity for organizations outside of the USA, but may point to an advertising mismatch of US-based economic development organizations' objectives with those of the magazines' readers.

Brochures

A brochure can summarize the positive attributes that a community wants to advertise into a tangible, take-away package. Glossy brochures, regardless of their contents, can impress an audience by hinting at the dedication and resources of a community necessary to put such packages together. Historically, brochures and business cards have also been used as a physical expression which serves to legitimize a person and/or organization. However, since the production of brochures is receiving a significant budget allocation by economic developers but receives one of the lowest effectiveness ratings, it raises doubt about the value of continuing this marketing practice. One influential corporate real estate site selector thinks they do not have much purpose other than proving that the organization exists. According to Bob Ady, "Brochures establish credibility, but serve little purpose otherwise."[16]

Brochures are often very general, trying to appeal to many audiences at once. A 2000 economic development study from the University of North Texas found that marketing activities "are increasingly conducted through the introduction of specific products and promotion of economic niches rather than exclusively with glossy brochures and trade shows."[17] The study also found that newer marketing approaches have been affected by national and subnational budget shortfalls since the 1970s, which have made communities rethink the use of expensive strategies like brochures.

A previous advantage of brochures was that they were often one of the few ways for organizations to physically hand something to prospective business investors at trade shows or during a meeting. However, in an increasingly online world, the ability to send digital brochures to someone you are physically talking to or the ability to access community websites online remotely through multi-media phones and Internet enabled PDAs is eliminating the comparative advantage brochures used to have. In addition, the professionalism and attractiveness of a community's website is becoming more important than any tangible product in establishing legitimacy. Since brochures cannot be updated in the same manner, communities that invest in them are often left with stockpiles of expensive, outdated documents that no longer reflect what the community wants to say about itself in the present.

In the past five years, economic development organizations reported on average that they scaled back their financing of television and radio advertising, print advertising, telemarketing, and videos (see Table 2-2). These strategies are scheduled to be cut again in the next five years. Contrary to strong general advertising trends, economic developers reported on average that they decreased spending on online advertising in the past five years, even though they planned to reverse this trend and increase spending in the next five years.

Table 2-2. Largest decreases in marketing budget

Marketing Strategy	Last 5 Years		Next 5 Years	
	Decreasing Budget	Increasing Budget	Decreasing Budget	Increasing Budget
Telemarketing	54%	8%	52%	9%
TV/radio advertising	52%	13%	44%	17%
Videos	43%	23%	36%	20%
Print advertising	36%	26%	34%	25%
Online advertising	36%	25%	29%	35%
Direct mail	28%	25%	24%	30%
Brochures	25%	27%	22%	26%
Trade shows and conferences	20%	42%	15%	42%
Targeted lead development databases	19%	34%	16%	42%
Slogans, logo and graphic identity	14%	38%	16%	28%
Out-of-town meetings with businesses	11%	52%	7%	59%
Site selection consultants and familiarization tours	11%	48%	8%	55%
Special events	11%	48%	10%	46%
Public relations	8%	47%	8%	49%
E-mail	5%	51%	6%	49%
Internet/website	4%	75%	3%	73%

Shaded strategies are those that decreased at a greater level than increased in the five year period.

Online Advertising

Only 1% of economic development marketing budgets is allocated toward online advertising, and only 13% of respondents identified it as an effective strategy. Furthermore, more economic developers reported cutting budget allocations for online advertising than raising them in the past five years.

This is dramatically different from the trends occurring in the larger US market of companies. North

American firms budget 10% of their marketing budgets to online advertising, roughly five times what economic development organizations spend.[18] Figure 2-2 maps the growth of online advertising revenues in the past eight years. Even after the dot-com bust at the end of 2000, the much publicized decline in Internet advertising was actually only a small dip. By the end of 2003, Internet advertising had surpassed its peak from the dot-com hey-day. Since the lowest quarter of spending during the dip of 2002, online advertising has grown over 400%. A study by IDC forecasts that from 2008 to 2012, Internet advertising is projected to grow at eight times the rate of advertising generally, doubling from $25.5 billion in 2007 to $51.1 billion in 2012. By 2012, it is expected to surpass newspapers and television (broadcast and cable) in terms of revenue.[19] Online advertising is growing because it works. Top level executives, according to Invesp Consulting, agree that online advertising provides the highest return on investment.[20]

Figure 2-2. Quarterly Revenue Comparisons, 2000-2007

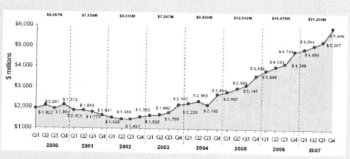

Source: PricewaterhouseCoopers/Interactive Advertising Bureau

Perhaps economic development marketing is uniquely unaffected by online advertising, but it is more likely that economic developers are lagging behind a strong advertising movement. In a discussion that came out of a recent training at the Southern Economic Development Council, many participants were confused and inquisitive as to why economic developers are not investing in online advertising at the same rate as organizations were investing in their websites. When asked about their own behavior, however, it was discovered that only a few in the room used Google AdWords, the most popular online keyword pay-per-click advertising tool. One of the key reasons explained as to why they were not using this service was because they didn't know how to use it.[21] Online advertising presents an opportunity for economic developers to invest in a growing marketing trend not recognized or used by many competing economic development organizations.

3. Industry Targeting and Scope

"The odds of hitting your target go up dramatically when you aim at it."

— Mal Pancoast

3. INDUSTRY TARGETING AND SCOPE

Any marketing program needs a clearly defined audience. An economic development organization should define the reach of its audience in terms of both geography and range of industries.

Survey respondents, as shown in Figure 3-1, tended to represent organizations that were at the city or county level. Only 4% were larger than statewide organizations. When asked to describe the geographic scope of their marketing efforts, however, the most frequent response was global at 29%, followed by nationwide at 27%. Clearly, the average economic development organization is responding to the forces of globalization and expanding the size of its target market area far outside the boundaries of its service area.

Figure 3-1. Organization service area vs. target market area

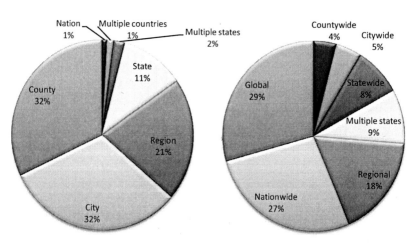

What is the area served by your organization?

What is the geographic scope of your marketing?

The changing nature of the global economy has had profound impact on the field of economic development and the industries it targets for future growth. Eva Klein writes, "We have entered a transition from the industrial economy to the global knowledge economy... a transformation as great as the one our society underwent about 200 years ago, when parts of the world's ubiquitous

24

agrarian economy entered the industrial economy."[22]   Within this shift to a knowledge economy in the United States, economic developers continue to focus on manufacturing as a targeted industry.

Table 3-1. Industries targeted by economic developers and site selectors (percent indicating industry as top 5 priority)

Industry	% Targeted by	
	Economic Developers	Site Selectors
Manufacturing	73%	49%
Information technology/high-technology	52%	35%
Business services	40%	43%
Distribution	40%	44%
Sciences (and life sciences)	38%	12%
Retail	30%	17%
Finance/insurance	23%	45%
Healthcare	22%	19%
Call centers	17%	41%
Agriculture	17%	1%

Economic developers were asked to name the five industries they spend the most time targeting, and site selectors/corporate real estate professionals were asked to name the five industries for which they most often need to locate space. Table 3-1 lists the top ten industries selected by economic developers and compares the ratings to those given by site selectors.

73% of economic developers selected manufacturing as one of their top five targeted industries, over 20% more than information technology/high-technology, the next most targeted industry. These results are surprising in light of the overall employment decline of the manufacturing sector nationwide, where employment dropped 20% from 1985 to 2005 (see Figure 3-2). This priority may be due to the political concerns in communities of keeping high-paying blue collar jobs in the midst of the national transformation to a service economy, which is highlighted in Figure C-3 in the Appendix. It should be noted, however, that declining employment does not equate to a dying industry. "Manufacturing employment has fallen and will likely continue to fall, but that does not mean investment will continue to fall," says Mark Sweeney of McCallum Sweeney. "For manufacturing to be competitive, it must be efficient with capital investments that are labor-saving. The investment to job ratio has increased. It is not unusual to have $1 million in investment per job, roughly double the ratio of ten years ago."[23]

Less than half of site selectors reported manufacturing as one of the top five industries for which they located space, though it still ranked as the number one source of clientele. The survey did not specify whether projects were within or outside of the United States.[24] It should be noted that not all companies needing to locate business real estate utilize the services of site selectors, as site selection consultants and corporate real estate professionals tend to serve companies that are large employers, are making a large financial investment, or have a high financial value. In particular, small businesses often lack the financial resources to hire a site selector. Industries that include a large share of small businesses may therefore be underrepresented in a site selector survey.

Many site selectors personally interviewed were hopeful about the future of manufacturing in the United States. "You look at the statistics and it's still by far the most active sector [for site selection consultants]," says Deane Foote of Jacobs Carter Burgess. "Overall it still has more projects than any other sector. Even though you read about it all going overseas, it's just not true."[25] The nature of manufacturing in the United States is certainly changing. "Low-cost manufacturing will continue to leave North America," explains Don Schjeldahl of the Austin Company, "but what's happening is that new technologies are leading to new markets, and a lot of these technologies require sophisticated manufacturing, customization, time sensitive manufacturing, or all those things, and you need highly skilled people."[26] Many site selectors interviewed pointed to alternative energy as a key source of new investment. Even many traditional manufacturers are realizing the benefits of staying local, such as just-in-time shipping. Dennis Donovan of the Wadley Donovan Group says that freight sensitive businesses, such as battery manufacturers, are expanding less overseas due to high transportation costs.[27] He explained that within the United States, manufacturing is locating in smaller communities because of lower operating and labor costs.

Site location is also a far more important decision for manufacturers than for most other industries. "Unlike retailers who can locate on every corner, manufacturers only site a new facility once in a great while," says Tim Monger of Colliers International. "There's more at stake for manufacturing than for any other industry, because they're investing a significant amount of money. It's quite a roll of the dice in setting up a new location and making sure you have a good location and labor pool."[28] This may further explain why experts in site selection are so involved in the location of manufacturing facilities. As a corollary, it is very possible that the focus of the site selectors owes more to manufacturing's highly complex logistical requirements than to the total amount of site selection decisions that companies are making in the different industries.

While economic developers focused more attention on manufacturing, information technology, and sciences, site selectors placed more emphasis on finance/insurance and call centers.[29] The survey participation of rural economic developers may help explain why finance and insurance were not targeted by economic developers as much as they were the focus of site selection professionals. This is further discussed in Section 5 of the book.

Figure 3-2. U.S. employment growth in selected industries, 1985-2005

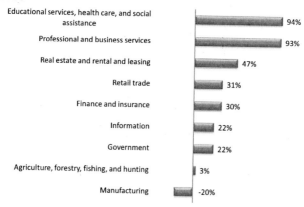

Educational services, health care, and social assistance	94%
Professional and business services	93%
Real estate and rental and leasing	47%
Retail trade	31%
Finance and insurance	30%
Information	22%
Government	22%
Agriculture, forestry, fishing, and hunting	3%
Manufacturing	-20%

Source: Bureau of Economic Analysis

4. Differences by Characteristics of Organizations and Communities

"Hawaii is a unique state...it is different from the other 49 states. Well, all states are different, but it's got a particularly unique situation."

– Dan Quayle

4. DIFFERENCES BY CHARACTERISTICS OF ORGANIZATIONS AND COMMUNITIES

Characteristics that define an economic development organization, both in terms of the structure of the organization itself as well as the characteristics of the community it serves, were found to impact the marketing approaches used.

ORGANIZATIONAL STRUCTURE

Government and economic development corporations (EDCs) were the most represented types of organizations in the survey. Although there is a negative stereotype of government being less effective and less able to keep up with modern practices of private sector organizations, the results of the survey show that this is not true for marketing within the economic development profession. In fact, government has embraced the most effective marketing strategies and is allocating more funds to the top two most effective strategies, Internet/websites and out-of-town meetings with businesses, than EDCs. In addition, government organizations prioritized new media (e.g. websites) over traditional media (e.g. print advertising) compared to EDCs, which are more private-sector in character. These priorities and allocations were not impacted by budget, as the median budgets for both EDCs and public organizations were the same. Public organizations also rated their marketing programs more effective than did EDCs. Chambers of Commerce, which represented about 9% of survey respondents, rated their marketing effectiveness higher than either government or EDCs (see Figure C-4 in Appendix). Though they budgeted the least for brochures, Chambers of Commerce budgeted similarly to EDCs for websites and print advertising (see Table C-5 in Appendix).[30]

Table 4-1. Average budget allocation of marketing strategies by organizational structure

Strategy	% of Budget Allocated by	
	EDCs	Government
Brochures	13%	9%
Direct mail	5%	4%
E-mail	3%	4%
Internet/website	13%	21%
Online advertising	1%	1%
Out-of-town meetings with businesses	8%	11%
Print advertising	13%	10%
Public relations	8%	8%
Site selection consultants and familiarization tours	6%	6%
Slogans, logo and identity	3%	3%
Special events	7%	7%
Targeted lead development databases	2%	3%
Telemarketing	0%	1%
Trade shows and conferences	12%	11%
TV/radio advertising	2%	1%
Videos	3%	2%

POPULATION SIZE/URBANITY

Results were analyzed by whether the service area was urban, suburban, or rural. Respondents were able to choose any or all of these classifications because many economic development organizations represent diverse geographies, but for the purpose of analysis, only the responses of organizations that represent one distinct area type were examined. It should be noted that a large population size does not necessarily indicate the presence of large communities, as it may rather mean that the organization's service area is very large and encompasses many small communities.

Relatively new strategies for some economic developers include focusing on industries and businesses that create amenities desired by the "creative class" and young professionals, which are becoming more widely part of the industry's discourse.[31] Small and rural areas were more likely than larger and more urban areas to prioritize the attraction of retail, food service/accommodation, and arts/entertainment.[32] Urban areas had a stronger orientation to targeting industries that create jobs for those in the knowledge economy, such as finance, science, and high-tech.[33] Smaller communities may feel that they cannot compete for knowledge-based industries because they lack workforces with the necessary skills and training, and are instead focusing on what they realistically feel they can attract.[34] Also, smaller areas may often be overlooked by retail and amenities that typically locate in larger cities, and therefore have to exert more effort in targeting them. They may also feel that building certain amenities will allow them to grow and attract new residents that can later fill jobs in the industries that larger areas target. Larger communities with many knowledge-based industries are typically already desirable locations for the creative class and young professionals, as well as retail and amenity businesses. Even though cities may desire new retail and amenities, they do not have to target them as aggressively and can focus efforts on attracting and retaining more professional industries.

Table 4-2. Industries targeted by size of population of service area (percent indicating industry as top 5 priority)

Industry	Population		
	Less than 25,000	25,000 to 100,000	Greater than 100,000
Accommodation and food service	34%	19%	7%
Agriculture	24%	18%	14%
Arts, entertainment, and recreation	24%	17%	8%
Business services	33%	39%	42%
Call centers	12%	20%	17%
Distribution	35%	46%	38%
Education	5%	6%	6%
Finance/insurance	3%	14%	32%
Healthcare	14%	23%	23%
Housing	23%	10%	6%
Information technology/high-technology	31%	44%	60%
Manufacturing	70%	76%	72%
Media	2%	2%	3%
Mining	4%	2%	2%
Public administration	6%	1%	3%
Real estate and Construction	18%	15%	14%
Retail	59%	46%	17%
Sciences	12%	24%	50%
Transportation	13%	19%	12%
Utilities	5%	4%	4%
Wholesale trade	13%	10%	7%

Even though budgeting for websites did not seem to be affected by population size of the service area, strictly rural areas, and to a lesser extent suburban areas, were found to spend a higher percentage of their budgets on websites than strictly urban areas.[35] Perhaps these less urbanized areas are discovering that having a strong online presence is essential to compete with the major, well-known cities.

Table 4-3. Average budget allocation of marketing strategies by urbanity of the service area

Strategy	Service Area Type		
	Rural	Suburban	Urban
Brochures	10%	11%	12%
Direct mail	5%	5%	5%
E-mail	3%	3%	4%
Internet/website	20%	17%	14%
Online advertising	1%	1%	1%
Out-of-town meetings with businesses	12%	9%	9%
Print advertising	11%	13%	13%
Public relations	7%	7%	9%
Site selection consultants and familiarization tours	6%	7%	5%
Slogans, logo and identity	3%	3%	3%
Special events	6%	8%	8%
Targeted lead development databases	3%	1%	3%
Telemarketing	0%	0%	0%
Trade shows and conferences	11%	11%	11%
TV/radio advertising	1%	1%	2%
Videos	1%	2%	2%

Only 30% of organizations serving strictly rural areas characterized their marketing programs as effective, while 51% of urban areas considered their marketing effective (see Figure C-5 in Appendix). This may be due to the budget limitations of smaller and rural organizations. Additionally, as the global economy shifts away from industries that have traditionally been the lifeblood of rural areas in the United States, organizations serving them may feel somewhat disillusioned with the results of their marketing efforts.

REGION

Figure 4-1. Regional boundaries for geographic comparison

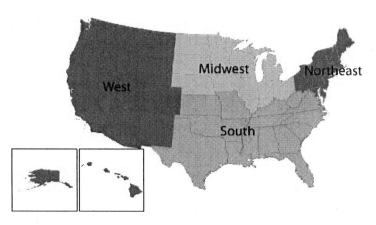

      Regional differences within the United States make the country a diverse and interesting place, but do those regional differences extend to economic development marketing? This study aimed to find out.

      As pictured in Figure 4-1, respondents were grouped into 4 different regions: West, Midwest, South, and Northeast, based on the general boundaries of the major regional economic development associations, even though these may not be the typical regional divisions of the nation.[36] Compared to the other regions, Midwestern respondents gave their own marketing programs low ratings in terms of effectiveness (see Figure C-6 in Appendix). At the same time, Midwestern organizations were found to spend the most of any region on websites (see Table C-6 in Appendix). Perhaps the challenges that Midwestern organizations face have forced them to quickly adapt to the most effective strategies and realize that having a good website is an effective way to begin raising awareness of a community so that they will be considered. However, as Table 4-4 shows, Midwestern communities are not responsible for the rural trend of amenity creation, as they were the least likely to target arts/entertainment and accommodation/food service, and only Northeastern organizations targeted retail less. These three industries were most heavily targeted by Western organizations. This may be the effect of measures like Proposition 13 in California, the ballot initiative that limited property taxes and forced the state to boost alternative government revenue generators such as sales tax. Northeastern organizations were the most likely to attract knowledge industries.[37]

Table 4-4. Industries targeted by region (percent indicating industry as top 5 priority)

Industry	Region			
	West	Midwest	South	Northeast
Accommodation and food service	21%	6%	13%	11%
Agriculture	20%	26%	11%	18%
Arts, entertainment, and recreation	17%	10%	10%	13%
Business services	42%	30%	43%	40%
Call centers	9%	21%	22%	13%
Distribution	25%	51%	49%	25%
Education	11%	4%	4%	3%
Finance/insurance	19%	24%	21%	40%
Public administration	3%	2%	3%	2%
Healthcare	24%	20%	21%	24%
Housing	11%	8%	11%	7%
Information technology/high-technology	52%	48%	51%	59%
Manufacturing	61%	85%	74%	76%
Media	3%	1%	3%	3%
Mining	3%	1%	3%	0%
Real estate and Construction	17%	16%	13%	15%
Retail	43%	23%	30%	16%
Sciences	32%	38%	39%	47%
Transportation	11%	20%	16%	6%
Utilities	5%	3%	4%	4%
Wholesale trade	9%	11%	8%	7%

5. Practices of Effective Organizations

"People seldom improve when they have no other model but themselves to copy after."

— Oliver Goldsmith

5. PRACTICES OF EFFECTIVE ORGANIZATIONS

We have thus far looked at how economic development organizations generally define their target audience, set their marketing budgets, and choose strategies, but what sets the organizations that have particularly effective marketing programs apart from the rest? The survey results contain some clues.

Respondents were asked to rate the effectiveness of their overall marketing programs and techniques. Those that rated themselves effective marketers were more likely to rate their local economies as experiencing growth (see Figure C-7 in Appendix). Perhaps these respondents were being optimistic in their responses to these two questions, or perhaps growing communities are better able to finance effective marketing campaigns. Another possible explanation is that effective economic development marketing results in economic growth. Because of these possibilities, the behavior of those effective marketers warrants further examination.

Effective marketing requires effort. Respondents that gave their own marketing high marks allocated 18% more staff time to the task than those who did not feel their marketing was effective (see Table 5-1). The median marketing budget for effective marketers ($99,000) was more than twice that of ineffective marketers ($40,000). Interestingly, there was virtually no difference between the budgeting allocations of effective and ineffective marketers. It seems that it is less important how an organization spends its marketing budget than how much they have to spend to begin with.

While it is tempting to determine how economic developers can increase the effectiveness of their marketing by working smart while streamlining costs, the importance of working hard by dedicating budget and staff time to successfully market a community should not be underestimated. The exception to this is where there are opportunities for economic developers to optimize their marketing by reducing or reallocating costs away from ineffective marketing strategies and moving them toward effective ones.

Table 5-1. Prioritization of economic development staff time (percent indicating activity as top-5 priority)

Staff Activity	Identified as a Priority by	
	Ineffective Marketers	Effective Marketers
Business attraction	78%	86%
Business expansion	79%	75%
Business retention	78%	72%
Marketing	42%	60%
Site selection assistance	45%	48%
Small business support	39%	29%
Workforce development	28%	28%
Redevelopment	27%	27%
Research	18%	20%
Public policy	20%	17%
Real estate development	21%	17%

Significant discrepancies existed between the industry targeting practices of effective marketers and ineffective marketers (see Table C-7 in Appendix), which largely echo those found between economic developers and site selectors. Effective marketers mirrored the priorities of site selectors by placing more emphasis on business services, the sciences, information technology, and financial services, while correspondingly placing less emphasis on manufacturing, retail, and agriculture.

GENERATION GAP

As previously discussed, changing technologies have had profound impacts on the field of economic development, yet many organizations have been slow to adjust their priorities to more effective marketing opportunities. Age may be a possible explanation, as older economic developers who predominate in leadership positions may be less comfortable with new technology communication tools than younger economic developers that have grown up with technology always around them.[38] Some differences were observed when comparing the responses of those less than 40 years of age with those aged 50 or older:

- Younger respondents rated the Internet as a more effective marketing tool, and gave lower marks to direct mail. This finding complements studies by the Pew Research Center which find that Internet usage declines as age increases (see Figure C-8 in Appendix). Younger respondents were also more likely to find online site selection tools helpful (see Figure C-9 in Appendix).[39]

- Younger respondents were more likely to rate their local economies as experiencing growth, and to give higher ratings to their overall marketing programs and techniques.

- Younger respondents also reported that the websites for their respective organizations were updated more frequently than was the case with the older cohort.

Although this survey did not include analysis of people being marketed to by age, there are indicators that the types of marketing that economic development organizations use will be received differently by the different generations they are targeting.[40] This will be especially important as communities target the attraction of workers to their areas.

EXAMPLES OF SUCCESSFUL MARKETING STRATEGIES

Several respondents had specific examples of marketing strategies that they wanted to share. Regional partnerships were often mentioned by practitioners as being effective, as were online strategies and public relations efforts to get free publicity for their work. Others merely wished to impart a few words of wisdom to the rest of the field. Some highlights:

- "Get your own business (City Hall) in order before promoting your city, so that if a fish bites, you can respond promptly and thoroughly."

- "Make your CEOs happy and they will market the region for you."

- "Don't sell yourself short- don't be afraid to say 'no thanks,' 'you're not the kind of business we are interested in' or to explain that the prospect's expectations are too high."

- "Spend marketing dollars on one on one meetings rather than print ads."

- "Get your community some exposure in an article in a professional publication."

- "Put everything online!"

- "It takes a combination of preparedness, effort and partnerships to create successful development."

- "Created a broker event that was NOT golf related and drew 60 brokers who had never attended an event before."

- "Pure hard work and consistent application."

- "E-marketing has been our most successful effort. Our contact list (reach) has grown 800% in only one year."

6. Outsourcing

"There are three ways to get something done: do it yourself, hire someone, or forbid your kids to do it."

— Mona Crane

6. OUTSOURCING

As we have already seen, the marketing strategies necessary for economic development are numerous. Outside contractors may be necessary to perform certain functions due to limitations such as the staff size of economic development organizations, internal expertise, or specialization of the strategy.

Figure 6-1. Effectiveness vs. outsourcing of marketing strategies

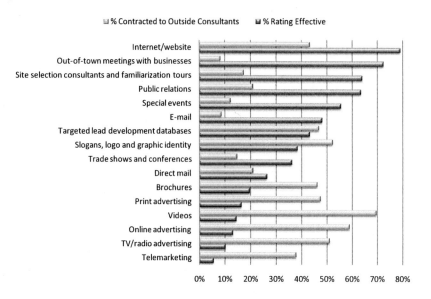

A comparison of those marketing strategies that were ranked effective and those that were outsourced, shown in Figure 6-1, reveals that the strategies that are ranked least effective generally have a stronger likelihood of being outsourced. The exception to this is the highest-rated strategy, Internet/website, which is outsourced far more often than the other highly rated strategies. Most of the strategies that are typically outsourced also constitute a small portion of the organization's marketing budget (see Table 2-1). The other notable exceptions to this trend are print advertising and brochures, which both have low effectiveness ratings and are typically outsourced, but also receive high budget allotments.

41

There are some possible explanations for this trend. Perhaps economic developers only work on something internally if they feel it is really effective and outsource anything they feel is not as effective. A second possible reason is that economic developers are bringing in outside expertise to work on the things they are least effective at implementing. A third possibility is that economic developers are allocating their valuable resources for outside experts into ineffective marketing strategies because they are under the false impression that that these marketing strategies are actually important and effective. This national survey suggests that low-value marketing strategies that are receiving valuable outside consulting resources are simply less effective, and may not be worth the price of outside consultants. A fourth reason, articulated by economic developers at an IEDC professional development training, is that the complexity of marketing requires that some strategies include both internal work and outsourcing, combined at different times in the marketing process.[41]

Among the most effective marketing strategies, three outliers experienced a high level of outsourcing: websites, targeted lead development databases, and slogans/logo/graphic-identity. It is worth noting that these strategies require relatively specialized skill sets to implement that don't typically fall within the expertise or job descriptions of economic development professionals. In the case of targeted lead development databases, implementation requires access to large databases of businesses and modeling systems to identify specific indicators for which businesses are better candidates to be targeted. In the case of slogans, economic developers may be able to develop taglines, but the associated graphics require graphic design expertise.

Similarly, websites may be outsourced because they are still a relatively new phenomenon for which organizations typically do not internally possess the necessary expertise to develop strategies to build and maintain their websites themselves. Also, unlike some of the more traditional marketing skill sets, websites are rapidly evolving in all industries and continue to require advanced technical skills to keep up with emerging online technologies. This may make outsourcing a more practical solution. An economic development organization may also consider it cheaper to outsource the development of its website than to build it internally under the incorrect notion that a website is a one-time investment, rather than a tool that must be constantly updated to best convey information about a community.

Websites are further complicated in this analysis because they are used by organizations for much more than just marketing. It is possible that, like many other private-sector companies, economic development organizations are going digital with more of their key business processes and accessing them online using third-party Software as a Service (SaaS) for things like document management, customer relations management (CRM), and project collaboration.[42] This reallocation of resources and services could also show up as an increase in the outsourcing budget for website services.

7. How Site Selectors Get Information

"Knowledge is of two kinds. We know a subject ourselves, or we know where we can find information on it."

– Samuel Johnson

7. HOW SITE SELECTORS GET INFORMATION

For economic development organizations working with site selectors, it is important to understand the behavior of these professionals.[43] How and when site selectors obtain information about communities matters. The results of our separate, parallel national survey shows that when researching communities, the top sources of information for site selectors and corporate real estate professionals are third-party data sources and economic development organization websites (see Figure C-10 in Appendix).[44] While economic development organizations may not have much influence over third-party data sources, they most certainly can influence their own websites.

Figure 7-1. Timing of contacts made by site selectors

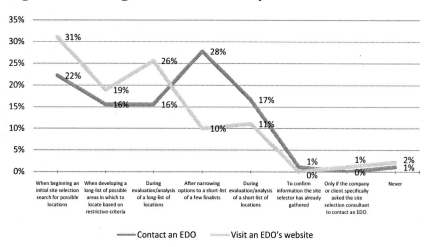

In the survey, site selectors were asked when, during the process of site selection, they would first contact an economic development organization and when they would first visit an economic development organization's website. Figure 7-1 indicates that in each of the first three stages of site selection, site selectors are far more likely to visit the website than make a phone call to the organization. Table 7-1 displays the same results cumulatively, where the total for each site selection stage includes the sum of all selection stages preceding it. By the end of the third stage of site selection (evaluating a long list of locations), **site selectors were almost one and a half times**

as likely to have visited economic development organization websites than to have personally contacted an organization. This also means that 43% of possible site selector "contact" is lost by not communicating effectively through the organization's website.

This is an important issue, because many communities and economic development organizations are being eliminated from the site selection process before they are ever contacted, which indicates the extreme importance of an effective website. One survey respondent wrote:

> "We often get calls from businesses that are already past the early state of their decision making process because they use our website tools to help them with their analysis. Because of our website our staff now spends more time with qualified and educated businesses instead of people that are just asking simple questions when they aren't even sure if they are going to invest in our community. For example, one business called and I started asking him basic questions and telling him about our community. He said, 'I know that stuff. I saw it on your website. I want you to set up a tour for me of three buildings that match what I need that I found on your website.'"

Table 7-1 reveals that 98% of site selectors use the websites of economic development organizations at some point in their research. This means that at least 98% of site selectors are using the Internet in some form for site selection research. Just as important, 99% of site selectors reported personally contacting an economic development organization at some point during the site selection process, confirming that economic development professionals do indeed add value to a community, as virtually everyone involved in site selection relies on their services. "Economic development organizations still comprise the lifeblood of site selection," says Dennis Donovan. "Once we're down to 10 or 15 potential locations per project, we reach out to economic development organizations before we have to visit local areas to find local operating conditions, such as what are the expanding companies, water and sewer capacity, electric power reliability, etc."[45]   Economic development organizations provide the qualitative information other sources lack.

Table 7-1. Timing of contacts (cumulative) made by site selectors*

Time of Contact	Economic Development Organization	Economic Development Organization's Website
When beginning an initial site selection search for possible locations	22%	31%
When developing a long-list of possible areas in which to locate based on restrictive-criteria	38%	50%
During evaluation/analysis of a long-list of locations	53%	76%
After narrowing options to a short-list of a few finalists	81%	86%
During evaluation/analysis of a short-list of locations	98%	97%
To confirm information the site selector has already gathered	99%	97%
Only if the company or client specifically asked the site selection consultant to contact an EDO.	99%	98%

* For every point in time, the totals up to and including that time are summed.

This survey complements a 2006 article by Bob Ady, the key results of which are summarized in Table 7-2.[46]   He found that within the six years previous to the study, the length of the typical site selection process shrank from over 6 months to only 4 to 8 weeks, which makes time a critical factor. Ady also found that the site selection process was typically involving more communities, that a much greater percentage of the process was being performed online, and that the primary tool for learning about communities had shifted from the personal visit to the Internet. Dennis Donovan explained that if he is looking to build a roster of information, "it's much more efficient to extract that data than to call 30 to 40 ED groups."[47]

According to Ady, "The site selection consultant uses the information from a community's website and other online sources. If a community doesn't have a website, the website cannot easily be found or it doesn't have the right type of information, the consultant moves on to other communities that have the information he or she needs."[48]

Table 7-2. The Internet's impact on site selection in 2006

Issue	Impact of Internet	
	5-6 Years Ago	2 Years Ago
Length of typical site selection search	6 months or more	4 to 8 weeks
Communities in initial screening	One or two dozen	Hundreds
Percentage of site selection process done in person	60%	20%
Percentage of site selection process done remotely	40%	80%
Number-one tool for learning about communities	Personal visit	Website/Internet

Source: Bob Ady, 2006

The results of the survey indicate that **a site selector's decision-making process about which communities make the short list of possible locations is based more on information gleaned from economic development websites than from personal contact with economic development organizations, and may not involve personal contact at all.** In addition to the ease of attaining information via the web, the often confidential nature of site selection decision-making gives the site selector further incentive for minimizing personal contact with the economic development organization in the early stages of the site selection process. A community that does not maintain a user-friendly website thus runs the risk of being eliminated from a location search without being given the chance to interact with the site selector personally. In such situations, the economic development organization would not even be aware that they could have been under consideration and that they might have helped their cause had they provided enough information online for a site selector to further the location search process in their community.

8. Website Features

"It would appear that we have reached the limits of what it is possible to achieve with computer technology, although one should be careful with such statements, as they tend to sound pretty silly in 5 years."

— John von Neumann (ca. 1949)

8. WEBSITE FEATURES

As the survey results have already demonstrated, both economic developers and site selectors find websites to be the most effective marketing strategy for economic development. Here we take a more in-depth look at the specific features of an economic development website.

Table 8-1. Most important features in an economic development website

Website Feature	% of Economic Developers Rating Feature as Important
Demographic reports	90%
Labor force	90%
Land/sites and buildings inventory	89%
Maps	86%
Staff directory and contact information	86%
Major industries or business/industry clusters	85%
Infrastructure	83%
Major employers	80%
Incentives	79%
Quality of life	76%
Employment training programs	76%
Site selection analysis assistance	75%
Hyperlinks to other organizations	71%
Business assistance services	68%
Testimonials and success stories	63%
News about community	62%
Comparisons to other areas	56%
Business list	51%
Transactions	45%
Videos	19%
User-generated content	11%

Respondents indicated that demographic reports were the most important element to include on a website, followed closely by information on the labor force, a land/sites and building inventory, and maps (see Table 8-1). The differences between the ratings of economic developers and site selectors can be seen in Table C-8 in Appendix.

Figure 8-1 lists the items that economic development organizations actually include on their websites. Standard items such as a staff directory/contact information and hyperlinks were included on the websites of almost all respondents, followed by maps and demographic reports. Information about assets of the communities, such as major employers, infrastructure, labor force, and quality of life amenities, was more likely to be part of a website than information on programs and services.

Though the current state of economic development websites may not be state of the art, the survey reveals that organizations are planning to make their websites more effective by adding enhanced features. The fastest-growing website features, which can be seen in more detail in Figure C-11 in Appendix, are site selection analysis assistance (integrated and interactive GIS, demographics, available properties, business analysis and dynamic maps), testimonials/success stories, and comparisons to other areas.

Figure 8-1. Website features and items

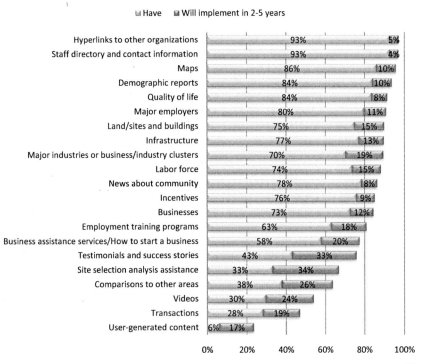

Today, economic development organizations tend to present their information in a static form rather than an interactive form (for more analysis on the presentation of static vs. interactive information, see Figure C-12 in Appendix). However, many organizations plan to implement interactive capabilities within the next 5 years, as seen in Figure 8-2. While only 33% of respondents have interactive maps, 39% more will implement this feature within 5 years. Within this same time frame, over a third aim to implement both interactive demographic reporting and interactive site selection assistance. When asked which website features are most important to be made interactive, economic developers indicated that interactivity is most important relating to land/sites and buildings inventory, followed by maps (see Figure C-13 in Appendix).

To put this in a broader context, this transition from static to dynamic is one that the broader Internet is experiencing across all industries. The older model of the Internet was composed of static websites that provided one-way communication: the website contained information and the website visitor viewed it. Websites are now more dynamic, serving as platforms that allow for interactive, two-way communication, often using dynamic tools, search, interactive features, and multi-media.[49]

Figure 8-2. Interactive features on economic development websites

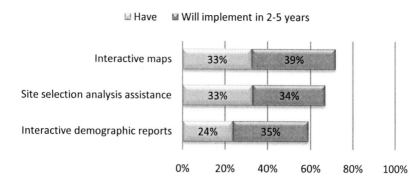

As can be seen from the graph, the amount of people that will add interactive mapping, site selection analysis, and demographic features is greater than the amount that currently has these interactive features, indicating that interactive economic development websites will experience dramatic growth. In the next few years, most economic development organizations will have interactive websites and only a minority will be left with static websites. An important implication of this trend is that, **within only a few years, interactive websites will provide this new majority of economic development organizations a competitive advantage** in website information analysis/communication over the remaining organizations that only have static websites.

ONLINE SITE SELECTION ANALYSIS

A significant technological development affecting the field of economic development recently has been the application of Geographic Information Systems (GIS) to online site selection tools, enabling powerful mapping and data analysis. As is seen in Figure 8-3, 81% of economic developers said that a GIS-based site selection tool is/would be helpful for their work. In the survey of site selectors, 77% found this technology valuable. Even given these highly favorable ratings, only a third of economic developers currently reported having such a system. Online GIS for site selection analysis will experience rapid growth in the next few years with 34% of economic developers indicating they will add it to their websites, which will make it a service provided by the majority of economic development organizations.

Figure 8-3. How helpful economic developers feel online site selection analysis technology using geographic information systems (GIS) would be for their work

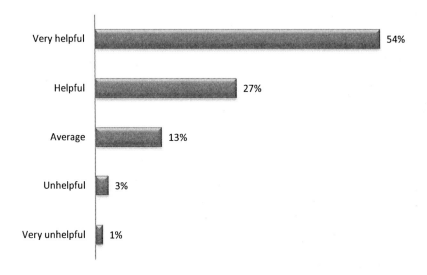

Site selectors were asked to choose which statements categorized their experiences with online site selection technology using GIS (see Figure C-14 in Appendix for full results). Over 30% indicated that they have been using this technology already and have found it helpful, and over half indicated that it makes their jobs easier by allowing them to access detailed information on their own time.

UPDATES

Given that economic development organizations rated the website as the most effective marketing tool, it is surprising that 45% of respondents reported that their website was updated monthly or less frequently (see Figure 8-4). A serious problem for economic developers trying to leverage the real-time value of websites as a marketing tool is that **9% of organizations only update their websites one or two times a year**. Even though most economic development professionals recognize the importance of the website as a marketing strategy, a significant percentage of them do not adequately ensure that the information on the site is updated to reflect their changing communities.

Figure 8-4. How often is your website updated?

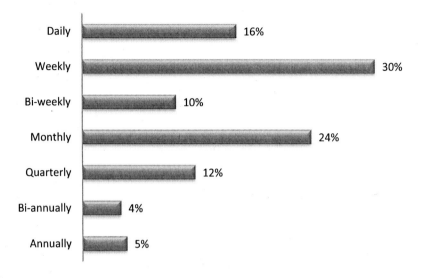

TRACKING

A website analytics service tracks visitor activity on a website, as well as where visitors are clicking from to get to the website. These services also communicate the percentage of visitors who leave a website without clicking any of the links, which is called a "bounce rate." A high bounce rate indicates a lack of effectiveness of a website/webpage. It may indicate that a website does not keep the attention of visitors or does not deliver what they are looking for. By analyzing the bounce rate, an organization can determine if a new element it added to its site in the past week, such as more intuitive organization of the links to different city departments, or a more pleasing graphical layout, is encouraging more visitors to explore the website in more detail.[50] Over 70% of respondents reported using a website analytics service (see Figure 8-5). While such services designed specifically for economic development do exist, most organizations use standard services. A dramatic problem is that **29% of economic development organizations do not use any service to track visitors to their website.** The fact that almost a third of organizations do not have any method for evaluating the

55

effectiveness of their websites, given their high effectiveness ratings and that virtually every organization maintains one, is alarming. It is even more concerning because online marketing is perhaps the most metric-measurable of marketing strategies and website analytics services can be found free of charge.

Figure 8-5. Methods for tracking visitors to economic development websites

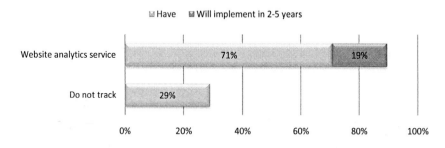

9. Benchmarking

"Measure what is measurable, and make measurable what is not so."

– Galileo Galilei

9. BENCHMARKING

Benchmarking the success of economic development efforts involves a unique set of measurements, as most marketing metrics revolve around the eventual sales of products or services. While economic developers can be thought of as "selling" their communities, there are no universally accepted standards for how to measure economic development marketing success.

Table 9-1. Criteria for benchmarking the success of an economic development organization (percent indicating measure as one of five most important criteria)

Benchmarking Criterion	% of Economic Developers Rating Criterion as Important
Jobs created	86%
Capital investment	70%
Announced projects	68%
Increased revenue and/or sales tax to government	52%
Increased wages and benefits	39%
Growth of economic output	33%
Decreased building vacancies and new real estate development	31%
Diversity of industry	28%
New quality of life/place amenities	17%
Workforce skills level increase	16%
Improvement of distressed neighborhoods	14%

Table 9-1 shows respondents pointed to job creation as the most important benchmark for the success of an economic development organization, followed by capital investment, announced projects, and increased government revenues. Job creation is a viable metric for benchmarking because organizations can quantify how many new jobs there are from a start-up, expansion or relocation and report that to a board of directors or elected officials. This benchmarking model is best aligned with an agricultural or industrial age where more employees result in more output, more revenue and more profit. Today, however, businesses may not need to add workers to achieve these goals. Instead, they may actually increase their profitability by decreasing the number of employees through automation and efficiencies. As a result, there is a clear difference, and perhaps a conflict, between the general benchmarking goals of economic developers (jobs) and the business community (profit).

Even though there is a growing demand for workforce availability and improved labor force skills, only 16% of economic developers felt that increasing the skill level of the workforce was an important benchmarking criterion. This lack of emphasis by economic development organizations may be because workforce development is often located in departments outside of economic development.

Table 9-2. Criteria for benchmarking the success of an economic development organization's marketing efforts (percent rating measure as most important criterion)

Benchmarking Criterion	% of EDs Rating Criterion as Most Important
Leads generated	35%
Awareness/recall of your organization	17%
Change of perception about community	15%
Number of businesses contacted	8%
RFPs sent to you	6%
Internet/website traffic	6%
Phone calls or e-mails to your organization	6%
Other	4%
Media coverage/mentions	2%

Table 9-2 shows respondents indicated very clearly that when it comes to evaluating their own marketing efforts, the generation of leads, which may result in business deals, is the most important criterion.[51] One respondent wrote, "We measure our marketing success via deals. If we aren't generating anything that looks like a deal, we are not here for long." The next two most highly rated criteria, "awareness/recall of the organization" and "change of perception about the community," are abstract concepts that are extremely difficult to measure in any systematic or easily implementable way. It is uncertain how economic developers measure these criteria or if they measure them at all. Additionally, there arguably is not necessarily a causal relationship between these criteria and actual economic investment in the community.

The "other" category received the second highest average rating, indicating that economic development organizations differ widely on how to benchmark marketing. Popular responses included site visits, proposals given, and company locations. Sadly, **the most common alternate response given by respondents was that their organizations did not benchmark their marketing in any way.**

Conclusion

"You've got to be very careful if you don't know where you're going, because you might not get there."

– Yogi Berra

CONCLUSION

The field of economic development is undergoing rapid change. Accelerating technology, says site selection consultant Ed McCallum, has left community and economic development at a crossroads, and communities have no excuse not to embrace this technology.[52] Delayed responses to the marketplace will be increasingly devastating to communities, as they attempt to market themselves to businesses that are increasingly footloose in a global economy, and whose business practices and preferences regarding site selection are ever-evolving. Communities must provide the information that businesses and corporate real estate professionals need because information is a competitive advantage. Also, the need for information intensifies as the economy worsens. Businesses and real estate professionals typically don't dig deep and ask as many questions when the economy is strong, but the demand for information rises as the economy deteriorates.[53]

The conditions and pressures of working in the public, quasi-governmental, and non-profit sectors may attribute to the delay of economic development organizations in adopting new technologies. Additionally, economic developers do not always budget according to what strategies they themselves perceive to be effective, further indicating the presence of a lag between awareness and action.

The profession has come a long way. Back in 1988, a study released in Economic Development Quarterly titled "Shoot Anything that Flies; Claim Anything that Falls" detailed findings from interviews with economic development practitioners. Practitioners reported that the uncertainty of how to properly promote a community led them to participate in programs with unpredictable consequences, for "to do something is better than to remain inactive."[54] The study's author commented that the economic development profession provides a challenging combination of the detailed scrutiny of the public sector with the risk and insecurity of the private sector. The advent of new technologies has opened up greater options for the profession, expanding the practitioner's choices for how to best promote a community. The results of the survey, however, reveal solid conclusions that may help reduce some of this uncertainty.

- Both economic developers and site selectors agree that an organization's website provides the most effective marketing strategy for economic development. It is the first point of contact that site selectors have with an organization, and by the third stage of the site selection process almost one and a half times as much communication was found to take place through the website than through personal contact. A comparison of marketing effectiveness and budget allotments revealed that websites are extremely cost effective, especially when compared to traditional strategies. One economic developer who responded to the survey commented, "Just because our organization is in a magazine doesn't mean everyone read it. Just because we have a special event doesn't mean that people didn't just come for the free food or booze. But you don't come to a website because it's fun. You come because you are interested in our economic development."

- Although websites are perceived as effective tools, most economic development organizations could do far more to increase their effectiveness. 29% still do not possess a website analytics service to track visitors to their websites, 45% fail to update their websites more than once a month, and 67% lack online site selection assistance.

- While it is undoubtedly necessary to develop an effective website, economic development organizations should also recognize the importance of personal, face-to-face interaction, which was valued highly by site selectors and economic developers alike. Ninety-nine percent of site selectors reported personally contacting an economic development organization during the process of site selection, demonstrating that the services of knowledgeable economic development staff are truly irreplaceable, no matter the advances in technology.

- Economic development organizations do not always prioritize their budgets in terms of what strategies they find effective. This is most evident in the case of print advertising, which received the second highest average budget allocation despite its low effectiveness rating. On the other hand, public relations, special events, site selection consultants/familiarization tours, and targeted lead development databases were all rated very effective, but were given relatively less money. Most marketers finance strategies that work well. Economic development organizations should be no different.

• Ineffective marketing strategies tend to be outsourced by economic development organizations. While there are several possible reasons for this practice, economic developers may want to reevaluate whether some of these strategies are worth investing in at all.

• Budgeting and industry targeting is significantly affected by the characteristics of the community served. Effective marketing strategies were utilized in certain types of organizations and areas more than others. These organizations tended to be small, rural, and in the Midwest. They also tended to be government organizations rather than economic development corporations. Smaller communities in the West focused on creating amenities, while larger communities in the Northeast targeted knowledge-based industries. Economic developers should be aware that different organizations face different challenges, but they should also be aware of how their own activities compare to similar organizations and communities.

• Targeting the manufacturing industry is the top priority of economic developers even though it is a declining employment sector. High-growth industries such as business services, information, and finance receive lower priority. Economic development organizations most commonly benchmark their success by the amount of jobs created. This appears to be in conflict with targeting manufacturing as the top industry. Looking forward, if employment continues to be the measure of success, successful economic developers must either place more emphasis on businesses in expanding employment industries or target the growing sub-segments of the manufacturing sector.

- Economic developers have not followed the larger trend toward online advertising that is seen in other industries. Only 13% of economic developers rated it as an effective strategy and it received only 2% of the marketing budget, even though most businesses allocate 10% of their budget to it, it is growing throughout other industries, and it is one of the most measurable forms of marketing. Respondents reported on average that they would increase budgeting for online advertising in the next five years, even though they cut funding within the past five years.

- Nothing comes for free, including effective economic development marketing. Economic developers who reported having effective marketing programs also reported devoting more staff time to marketing, as well as having significantly higher marketing budgets. Those who reported having effective marketing reported having stronger local economies on average.

- Effective marketers also exhibit particular tendencies in their targeting of industries. Compared to the average organization, they target more of their marketing efforts at business services, sciences, information technology, and financial services, and focus less on manufacturing, retail, and agriculture. These preferences are closely aligned with the needs of the site selection professionals surveyed.

- The most common standard for benchmarking the success of an economic development organization's marketing efforts is the number of leads generated, which is a measurable criterion. On the other hand, organizations almost as commonly judge marketing effectiveness through immeasurable criteria, or do not benchmark their marketing at all. If economic development organizations want to be able to prove their marketing value, this is a trend that will need to end.

Every community has something to offer, and economic development practitioners must be experts in communicating what that "something" is. We live in a time when the methods of communication are changing rapidly. Practitioners that can best adjust to these changes will be in the best position to help their communities thrive.

ACKNOWLEDGMENTS

No book is the work of just one person, or, in this case two people. We are very thankful to the people that took the time to support the creation of this book.

We especially would like to thank the University of California at Berkeley's Department of City and Regional Planning for agreeing to participate and oversee this study. At UC Berkeley we would like to specifically thank Dr. Karen Chapple, Associate Professor of City & Regional Planning and the Faculty Director for the Center for Community Innovation for reviewing the writing and providing guidance throughout the survey design, implementation and analysis. We would also like to thank Catherine Sutton for making the university's facilities available to us to present this research and broadcast our finding through a webinar.

At GIS Planning we thank Pablo Monzon, Co-founder of the company, for his support of this project, especially as it took staff (and the other co-founder's) time and resources away from day-to-day activities. Thank you for supporting this project and trusting that this project would not only make the company smarter but also the whole profession. Additional thanks are due to Mario Ubalde and Chad Catacchio who both gave valuable insights into the writing and editing of the book.

We would also like to thank the people that gave tremendous feedback as early or partial iterations of this book were shared or presented including Rebecca Ryan of Next Generation Consulting, Dean Whittaker of Whittaker Associates, and the many economic developers that provided public feedback at economic development conferences and trainings for organizations like the International Economic Development Council, Southern Economic Development Council and American Chamber of Commerce Executives.

Special thanks is given to Agnes Briones Ubalde who endured her husband working late nights to get this book done.

This research would not have been possible without the assistance of the national, state and regional economic development member associations that had their members participate in the survey, all of which are named in Table A-1 of the Appendix.

Appendices

APPENDIX A: CHARACTERISTICS OF ECONOMIC DEVELOPERS SURVEYED

The University of California at Berkeley distributed a survey to economic developers through economic development member organizations at the state, regional and national level. It is estimated that the number of economic developers that received the survey is between 7,000 and 10,000. The survey received 1,064 responses, of which 601 were complete. Since the survey was also delivered to the individual respondents by the member organizations, it was not possible to determine the exact response rate. The length of the survey, which was approximately 15-20 minutes, was a major reason for the large number of partial responses. These partial responses were analyzed along with the complete responses, resulting in differing sample sizes for different questions.

Figure A-1. Respondents by state

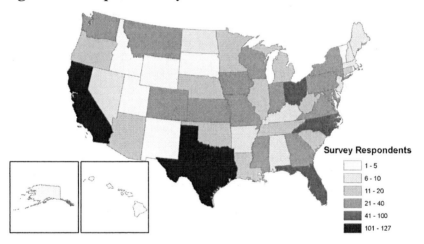

All 50 states were represented in the survey. The most heavily represented states included some of the most populated states. California had 127 respondents, followed by Texas with 105 respondents and Florida with 61 respondents.

Table A-1. State and regional association members represented

Arizona Association for Economic Development
Arkansas Economic Developers
California Association for Local Economic Development
California Association for Local Economic Development
Connecticut Economic Development Association
Economic Developers of North Dakota
Economic Development Association of Alabama
Economic Development Association of Minnesota
Economic Development Association of New Jersey
Economic Development Council of Colorado
Economic Development Council of Maine
Florida Economic Development Council
Georgia Economic Development Association
Illinois Development Council
Indiana Economic Development Association
Kansas Economic Development Alliance
Kentucky Industrial Development Council
Louisiana Industrial Development Executives Association
Maryland Economic Development Association
Massachusetts Economic Development Council
Michigan Economic Developers Association
Mid-America Economic Development Council
Mississippi Economic Development Council

Missouri Economic Development Council
Montana Economic Developers Association
Nebraska Economic Developers Association
New Hampshire Economic Developers Association
New York State Economic Development Council
North Carolina Economic Development Association
Northeastern Developers Association
Ohio Development Association
Oklahoma Economic Development Council
Oregon Economic Development Association
Pacific Northwest Economic Development Council
Pennsylvania Economic Development Association
Professional Developers of Iowa
South Carolina Economic Developer's Association
Southern Economic Development Council
Tennessee Industrial Development Council
Texas Economic Development Council
Vermont Economic Development Authority
Virginia Economic Development Association
Washington Economic Development Association
West Virginia Economic Developers Council
Wisconsin Economic Development Association
Wyoming Economic Development Association

Figure A-2. Describe the experience of your area's economy compared to the economic growth for the nation.

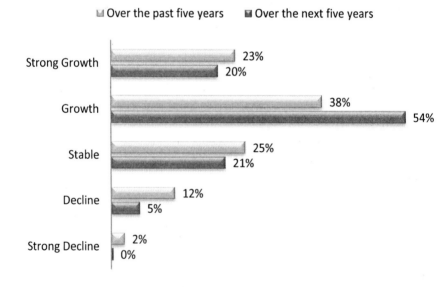

The survey respondents were largely optimistic about the future of their communities, predicting growth levels for their service areas that were higher than what the growth levels had been on average for the five years previous.

Figure A-3. What is the population of your service area?

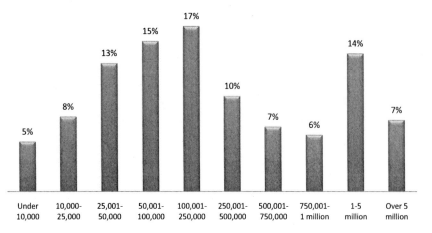

The organizations of survey respondents varied considerably in population service area. 45% of survey respondents serviced populations between 25,000 and 250,000. 21% serviced populations of over 1 million.

Figure A-4. How would you describe the character of the area served by your organization?

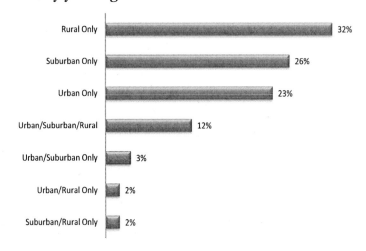

The survey responses were fairly proportionally distributed between rural, suburban and urban areas. 40% had some urban character, 43% had some suburban character, and 48% had some rural character. 12% of respondents indicated that the character of the area served included all three geographic types, which were likely organizations servicing large regions or states.

Figure A-5. What is the structure of your organization?

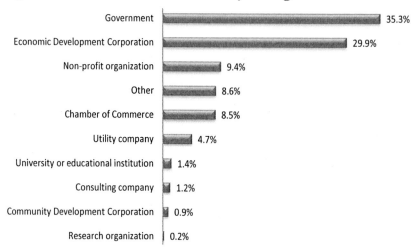

35% of respondents represented government agencies, followed by 30% representing economic development corporations. Chambers of Commerce and non-profit organizations each comprised 9% of the responses.

Figure A-6. My position in the organization

While there was some variation in the positions of those who took the survey, 89% of respondents were managers or executives in their organizations.

Figure A-7. My age

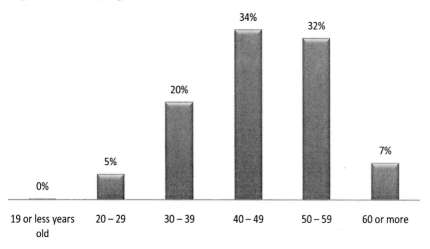

Given the dominant representation of senior-level professionals in the survey, it is not surprising that the majority of the respondents (75%) were over 40 years in age. The over 60 cohort (7%) had greater representation than the below 30 cohort (5%). There was only one respondent with an age of 19 years or less.

Table A-2. What national and international associations are you or your organization a member of? (Top ten associations listed)

Association	% of Respondents Claiming Membership
International Economic Development Council	77%
CoreNet Global	30%
International Council of Shopping Centers	23%
Economic Development Institute	19%
Council for Community and Economic Research	17%
American Chamber of Commerce Executives	13%
Industrial Asset Management Council	12%
Urban Land Institute	12%
American Planning Association	11%
National Association of Industrial and Office Properties	10%

77% of respondents indicated affiliation with the International Economic Development Council, by far the most represented organization. CoreNet Global, International Council of Shopping Centers, and the Economic Development Institute also displayed strong representation.

APPENDIX B: CHARACTERISTICS OF SITE SELECTORS SURVEYED

UC Berkeley distributed a survey to 2,500 prominent site selection consultants and real estate professionals. The survey received 104 responses, 80 of which were complete. This represents a 4% response rate. This survey is a complement to the economic developer survey, and was significantly shorter. It was also distributed to fewer respondents as there are fewer site selection advisers than economic developers. As with the economic developer survey, partial responses were analyzed along with the complete responses, resulting in differing sample sizes for different questions.

Table B-1. Companies participating in site selector survey

Alvarez and Marsal	General Services Administration	Outsourcing Solutions Inc.
American International Realty Corp.	Gesch Property Management & Investments, LLC	The Pathfinders
The Austin Company	GlobeSite	Pizzuti Solutions LLC
BASF	GMAC ResCap	PMC - Sierra Inc.
Boeing Realty Corp.	Google	Pollina Corporate Real Estate, Inc.
Brian Wishneff & Associates	Green Tree Servicing LLC	Procter & Gamble Co.
Business Facility Planning Consultants, LLC	Grosvenor Management Consulting	RBC Dain Rauscher & Capital Markets
CA Commercial Realty Partners	GVA Hungary Kft.	Retriever Payment Systems
Cadence Design Systems Inc.	Humana Inc.	Sherwin-Williams Co.
Canup & Associates, Inc.	Jacobs Carter Burgess	The Staubach Company
CB Richard Ellis	J.P. Morgan Services India Pvt. Ltd.	Stewart Lawrence Group
Cisco Systems	JDS Uniphase Corporation	Studley, Inc.
Colliers Arnold	Johnson Controls, Inc.	Sun Microsystems
Colliers Houston & Co.	Jones Lang LaSalle	Suncorp
Colliers International	Juniper Network Inc.	Swinerton Builders
Concentra	Kaiser Foundation Health Plan, Inc.	Szatan & Associates
CresaPartners	Kaman Industrial Technologies	Taimerica Management
Crum & Forster	KLG	TEVA Pharmaceutical Industries Ltd.
Cushman & Wakefield	Land Advisors Organization	Toyota Motor Sales USA Inc.
DataNet, Inc.	Leak-Goforth Company, LLC	Trammell Crow Co.
DCG Corplan Consulting LLC	Location Advisory Services	Tyco Electronics
Deloitte Consulting LLP	Marvell Semiconductor, Inc.	Urdang Capital Management
eBay	McCallum Sweeney Consulting	The Vercitas Group
Expedia Inc.	Media General Inc.	Verizon
Express Scripts, Inc.	Mike Barnes Group, Inc.	Washington Mutual
Federal Mogul Corporation	Mohr Partners	Waste Management Inc.
Flynn Strategic Consulting	NAI MLG Commercial	Wilmington Trust
Frito-Lay Inc.	Newmark Knight Frank	World Business Advisors LLC

Figure B-1. What is the area served by your organization?

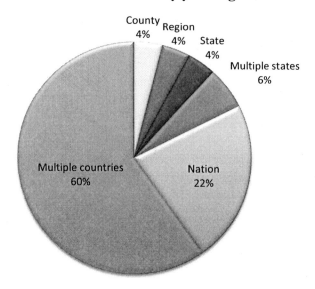

60% of site selectors surveyed served businesses in multiple countries, while an additional 22% served businesses nationwide.

Figure B-2. What are the geographic characteristics of the areas served by your organization?

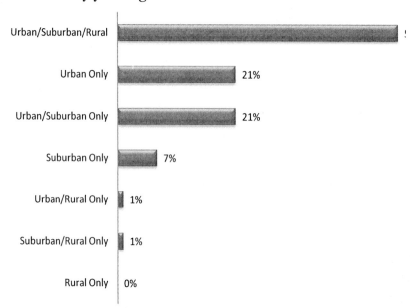

Site selector respondents had an urban orientation. 21% represented only urban areas, while no respondents represented only rural areas. This is in sharp contrast to the survey of economic developers, where the largest category of respondents (32%) represented solely rural areas.

Figure B-3. My role in site selection

49% of site selector respondents were corporate real estate professionals, versus 32% for site selection consultants. Real estate agents and brokers constituted another 11%.

Figure B-4. My position in the organization

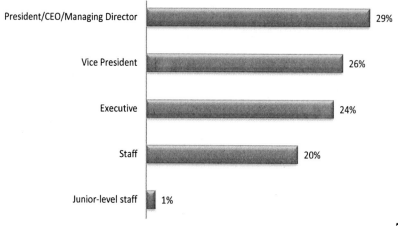

79% of site selector respondents were senior level, a level consistent with that of the economic developer survey.

Figure B-5. My age

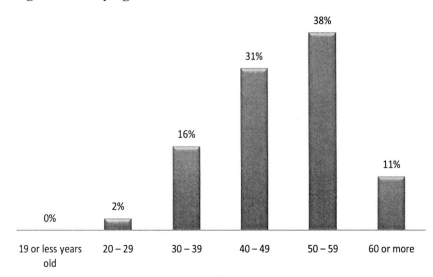

82% of site selectors were 40 years of age or older, including 49% over the age of 50.

APPENDIX C: ADDITIONAL CHARTS AND TABLES

Table C-1. The most effective marketing strategies used by economic development organizations (Percent of economic developers and site selectors rating effective)

Marketing Strategy	% of Respondents Rating Strategy Effective	
	Economic Developers	Site Selectors
Internet/website	79%	85%
Out-of-town meetings with businesses	72%	51%
Site selection consultants and familiarization tours	64%	69%
Public relations	64%	43%
Special events	56%	45%
E-mail	48%	31%
Targeted lead development databases	43%	48%
Slogans, logo and identity	38%	11%
Trade shows and conferences	36%	42%
Direct mail	26%	19%
Brochures	20%	19%
Print advertising	16%	9%
Videos	14%	7%
Online advertising	13%	4%
TV/radio advertising	10%	2%
Telemarketing	6%	4%

Figure C-1. Total Annual Ad Revenue for Site Location Magazines, 2002-2007

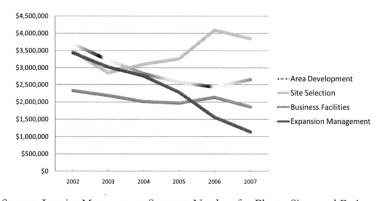

Source: Inquiry Management Systems. No data for Plants, Sites, and Parks.

Table C-2. Site Location Magazine Circulation, June 2007

Publication	Qualified Circulation	Paid Circulation
Site Selection	43,835	355
Area Development	43,456	0
Expansion Management	41,500	0
Business Facilities	43,000	0

Source: BPA Worldwide

Figure C-2. Total Site Location Magazine Circulation by Type

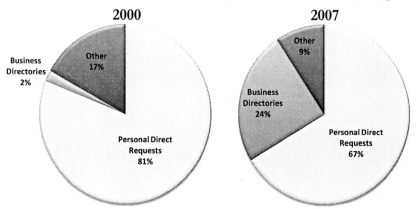

Source: BPA Worldwide

Table C-3. Total Site Location Magazine Circulation by Type

Publication	Circulation in December, 2000			Circulation in June, 2007		
	Personal Direct Requests	Business Directories	Other	Personal Direct Requests	Business Directories	Other
Site Selection	89%	8%	3%	70%	29%	1%
Area Development	63%	0%	37%	52%	47%	2%
Expansion Management	98%	0%	2%	75%	0%	25%
Business Facilities	75%	0%	25%	69%	20%	11%

Source: BPA Worldwide

The BPA Worldwide statistics show a dramatic increase in circulation from business directories (like Dun & Bradstreet) during the years from 2000 to 2007. During this period *Area Development* increased its circulation from non-personally directed requests from 0% in 2000 to 47% by 2007, giving it the highest percentage of recipients that had not personally requested the magazine.

Table C-4. Site Location Magazine Readership by Industry, June 2007

Publication	Manufacturing	% of Readership Working in Transportation Distribution and Warehousing	Business Services	Other
Site Selection	80%	2%	16%	2%
Area Development	78%	9%	9%	5%
Expansion Management	64%	2%	0%	33%
Business Facilities	54%	3%	38%	5%

Source: BPA Worldwide

A noticeable difference between the magazines' readership by industry is that *Business Facilities* has significantly more "Business Services" readership. Because economic developers are targeting job-growth as the top benchmark of their organizational success and because jobs in the service industry are growing significantly faster than the manufacturing industry (see Figure C-3), *Business Facilities* may be the best positioned to leverage their readership difference as an advantage for economic development organizations that advertise in its magazine.

Figure C-3: U.S. employment in manufacturing vs. services, 1985-2005 (millions of employees)

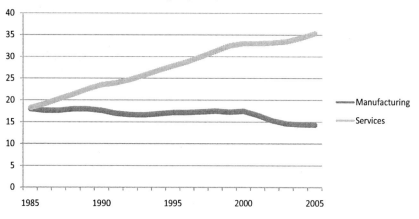

Source: Bureau of Economic Analysis

Figure C-4. Effectiveness ratings of overall marketing programs and techniques by organizational structure

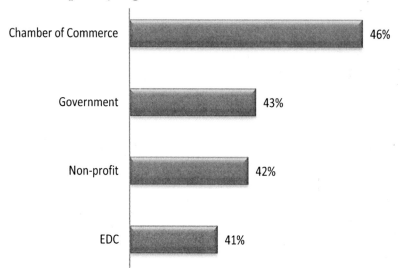

Table C-5. Average budget allocation of marketing strategies by organizational structure

	Organization Type			
Strategy	EDC	Government	Nonprofit	Chamber of Commerce
Brochures	**16%**	**10%**	**10%**	**9%**
Direct mail	8%	6%	7%	8%
E-mail	5%	6%	7%	5%
Internet/website	**15%**	**22%**	**18%**	**15%**
Online advertising	2%	1%	3%	4%
Out-of-town meetings with businesses	11%	14%	16%	15%
Print advertising	**17%**	**12%**	**15%**	**16%**
Public relations	10%	11%	9%	10%
Site selection consultants and familiarization tours	8%	9%	8%	7%
Slogans, logo and identity	5%	5%	5%	4%
Special events	9%	9%	10%	8%
Targeted lead development databases	3%	5%	3%	2%
Telemarketing	1%	1%	1%	1%
Trade shows and conferences	15%	13%	10%	13%
TV/radio advertising	3%	2%	2%	2%
Videos	5%	3%	3%	3%

Figure C-5. Effectiveness ratings of overall marketing programs and techniques by urbanity of the service area

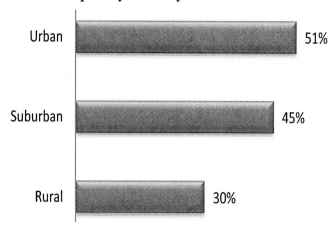

Figure C-6. Effectiveness ratings of overall marketing programs and techniques by region

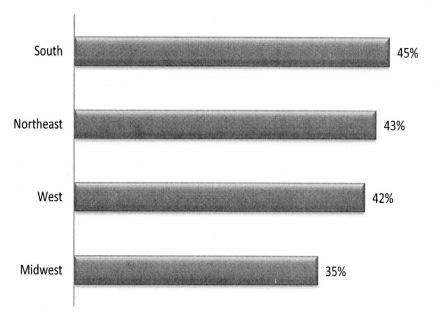

Table C-6. Average budget allocation of marketing strategies by region

	Region			
Strategy	West	Midwest	South	Northeast
Brochures	**12%**	**9%**	**11%**	**9%**
Direct mail	6%	5%	5%	4%
E-mail	3%	5%	3%	5%
Internet/website	**17%**	**21%**	**16%**	**19%**
Online advertising	1%	2%	1%	2%
Out-of-town meetings with businesses	9%	10%	12%	9%
Print advertising	11%	11%	11%	12%
Public relations	**11%**	**7%**	**7%**	**6%**
Site selection consultants and familiarization tours	5%	6%	7%	6%
Slogans, logo and identity	3%	3%	3%	3%
Special events	7%	6%	7%	9%
Targeted lead development databases	2%	2%	2%	2%
Telemarketing	1%	0%	1%	1%
Trade shows and conferences	11%	10%	11%	10%
TV/radio advertising	1%	1%	1%	2%
Videos	1%	1%	2%	1%

Figure C-7. Organizations experiencing strong growth

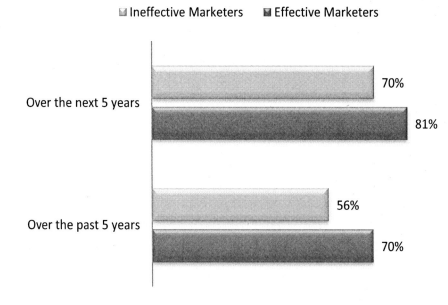

🗎 Ineffective Marketers 🗎 Effective Marketers

Over the next 5 years — 70% / 81%

Over the past 5 years — 56% / 70%

Table C-7. Targeted industries of effective marketers (percent indicating industry as top 5 priority)

Industry	% Identifying Industry as a Priority	
	Ineffective Marketers	Effective Marketers
Manufacturing	75%	72%
Information technology/high-technology	51%	54%
Business services	36%	47%
Distribution	38%	43%
Sciences	35%	41%
Retail	33%	29%
Finance/insurance	22%	25%
Agriculture	21%	13%
Wholesale trade	12%	6%

Figure C-8. Internet Usage by Age, 2007

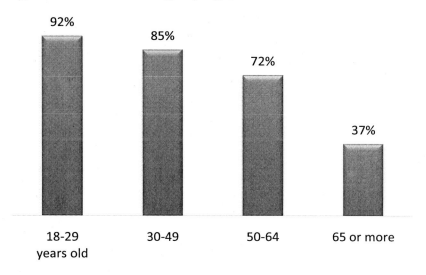

92%	85%	72%	37%
18-29 years old	30-49	50-64	65 or more

Source: Pew Research Center

Figure C-9. Effective marketing strategies by age of respondent

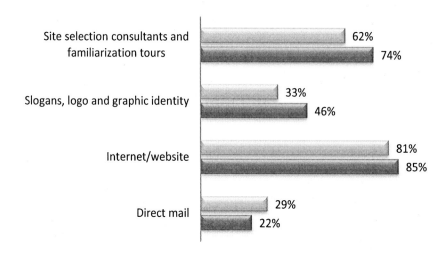

Figure C-10. How site selectors typically gather information about communities

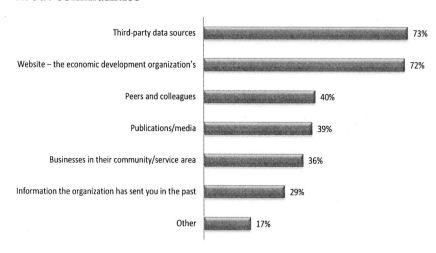

Table C-8. Useful/important features for economic development websites

Website Feature	% of EDs Rating Feature as Important	% Site Selectors Rating Feature as Useful
Demographic reports	90%	85%
Labor force	90%	83%
Incentives	79%	79%
Infrastructure	83%	77%
Land/sites and buildings inventory	89%	75%
Major employers	80%	75%
Maps	86%	74%
Major industries or business/industry clusters	85%	66%
Site selection analysis assistance	75%	64%
Staff directory and contact information	86%	62%
Quality of life	76%	62%
Comparisons to other areas	56%	54%
Employment training programs	76%	51%
News about community	62%	41%
Business list	51%	40%
Transactions	45%	31%
Hyperlinks to other organizations	71%	24%
Testimonials and success stories	63%	21%
Business assistance services	68%	17%
Videos	19%	7%
User-generated content	11%	6%

Figure C-11. Fastest growing features and items on economic development websites (greatest percentage that will be implemented in 2-5 years)

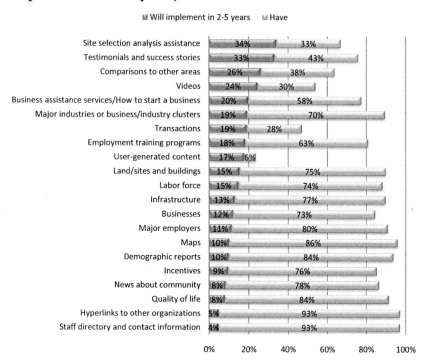

Figure C-12. How economic development organization websites provide information

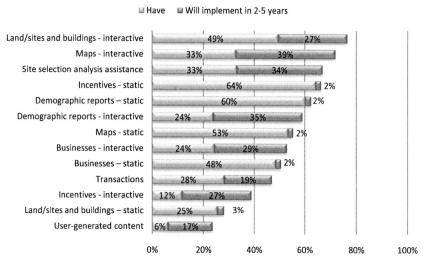

Legend: ⌷ Have ⌷ Will implement in 2-5 years

Category	Have	Will implement in 2-5 years
Land/sites and buildings - interactive	49%	27%
Maps - interactive	33%	39%
Site selection analysis assistance	33%	34%
Incentives - static	64%	2%
Demographic reports – static	60%	2%
Demographic reports - interactive	24%	35%
Maps - static	53%	2%
Businesses - interactive	24%	29%
Businesses – static	48%	2%
Transactions	28%	19%
Incentives - interactive	12%	27%
Land/sites and buildings – static	25%	3%
User-generated content	6%	17%

Figure C-13. How important economic developers feel it is to have the following items be interactive on an economic development website (percent rating important)

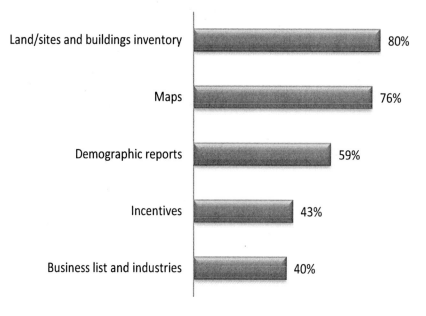

Category	Percent
Land/sites and buildings inventory	80%
Maps	76%
Demographic reports	59%
Incentives	43%
Business list and industries	40%

Figure C-14. Site selectors' experience with online GIS technology (respondents chose as many statements as were applicable)

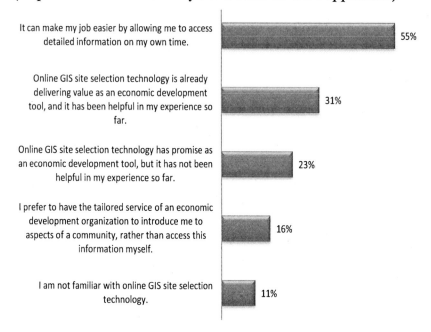

Table C-9. Criteria for benchmarking the success of an economic development organization's marketing efforts (percent rating measure as one of five most important criteria)

Benchmarking Criteria	% of Respondents Rating Criteria Important
Leads generated	82%
Awareness/recall of your organization	73%
Internet/website traffic	65%
Change of perception about community	57%
Phone calls or e-mails to your organization	55%
Number of businesses contacted	53%
Media coverage/mentions	49%
RFPs sent to you	41%
Other	8%

The question for benchmarking marketing asked organizations to rank their top five criteria, allowing for analysis on how organizations weighted their choices. Due to the large number of answer choices for the separate question for benchmarking overall success, organizations were asked only to select their top five criteria. This table displays the criteria for benchmarking marketing in a similar format to Table 9-1, which displays criteria for benchmarking overall success.

ABOUT THE AUTHORS

Anatalio Ubalde is Co-founder and President at GIS Planning Inc. and is CEO of ZoomProspector.com. Mr. Ubalde works with organizations throughout the nation to foster enhanced economic development strategies using Internet technology. His company's online product services are implemented across the USA and serve the majority of the 50 largest cities in the United States as well as numerous states and small communities. For the past two years GIS Planning has made the INC. 5000 list of fastest growing private companies in the United States. His work is featured in The Wall Street Journal, Los Angeles Times, TechCrunch, and the U.S. Department of Commerce "Innovative Local Economic Development Programs". Mr. Ubalde is on the Board of Directors for the International Economic Development Council and is a past recipient of the IEDC Outstanding Economic Developer of the Year Award. He was also a finalist for the Stockholm Challenge Award. Mr. Ubalde is frequently invited to advise about the use of Internet, marketing and GIS for economic development at national and international conferences making presentations on this subject throughout North America, Europe and Asia. He previously worked in local economic development with a focus on downtown revitalization, waterfront redevelopment, business attraction/expansion, business retention, and site selection assistance. He has a Masters degree in City Planning from U.C. Berkeley. Mr. Ubalde is an eight-time United States Master's Diving National Champion in springboard diving and All-American. In 2006 he won a bronze medal in springboard diving at the Masters World Championships. He is married to Agnes Briones Ubalde and is the father of Anatalio C. Ubalde, IV.

Eric Simundza has a background in economic development, workforce development, and land use planning. He holds a masters degree from the Department of City and Regional Planning at the University of California at Berkeley. As a Fellow at UC Berkeley's Center for Community Innovation, he worked on several projects, including a retail mix and retail leakage analysis for the Temescal Business Improvement District, a study of changing poverty concentrations in cities and suburbs along with the response of poverty-related community organizations, and a study of the effect of industrial zoning on business start-up and location patterns in California's Bay Area. Previously he worked for Seedco, an economic development nonprofit in New York City, where he helped a network of community organizations manage employment service programs.

ENDNOTES

1. An online survey was distributed to members of economic development organizations nationwide. Over 1,000 people responded, representing all 50 states. For further information, see Appendix A.

2. The word "community" is used extensively within this document and generally can be used interchangeably with other geographic descriptions including: area, city, county, state, and region.

3. For more information about this trend read: Ubalde, Anatalio. "Economic Development Dinosaurs vs. Fast Internet Information." *Economic Development America*, Spring 2007.

4. Ratings were rounded to the nearest whole number. Site selection consultants and familiarization tours rated 64.1% which was slightly higher than public relations at 63.6%.

5. These differences between the ratings of site selectors and economic developers are all significant at the 95% confidence level, except for the difference in the ratings of print advertising, which is significant at the 90% confidence level.

6. Psychologists refer to the tendency of people to overestimate their abilities as the better-than-average or "Lake Wobegon" effect. For more information, read Kruger, Justin, and David Dunning. "Unskilled and Unaware of It: How Difficulties in Recognizing One's Own Incompetence Lead to Inflated Self-Assessments." *Journal of Personality and Social Psychology*, 1999: 1121-1134.

7. Farris, Paul, Neil Bendle, Phillip Pfeifer, and David Reibstein. Marketing Metrics: *50+ Metrics Every Executive Should Master.* Upper Saddle River, NJ: Wharton School Publishing, 2006.

8. Sanders, Heywood. *Space Available: The Realities of Convention Centers as Economic Development Strategy.* Washington, DC: Brookings Institution, 2005.

9. Karpinski, Richard. "Recorded Web Events Click; On-Demand Events Better at Converting Registrants to Qualified Sales Leads." *BtoB* 90, no. 5 (2005): 28.

10. Elliott, Stuart. "Troubling '07 Forecast for the Old-Line Media but Not for the Online." *New York Times*, December 5, 2006.

11. Ibid.

12. Data on the circulation and advertising pages of these magazines comes from two sources. BPA provides data on circulation. Inquiry Management Systems provides information about advertising pages and revenue.

13. Circulation Audits, 2000-2007. *BPA Worldwide*. http://www.bpaww.com/library/index.cgi.

14. Ibid.

15. There are many examples of site location publications writing about opening facilities outside of the United States, including:

    – Reveler, Norma. "Around the World." *Business Facilities*, October 2005.

    – Crawford, Mark. "Expanding Options in Overseas Markets." *Area Development*, December 2007.

    – Semple, Alison. "Global Business Climate: Partly Sunny." *Site Selection*, November 2002.

16. Szuda, Stephanie. "Summit focuses on job struggles in the Illinois Valley" *The Times*, May 23, 2008. http://mywebtimes.com/archives/ottawa/display.php?id=360365

17. McGuire, Michael. "Collaborative Policy Making and Administration: The Operational Demands of Local Economic Development." *Economic Development Quarterly* 14, no. 3 (2000): 278-291.

18. ZenithOptimedia. "Quarterly Advertising Expenditures Forecasts." March 2008

19. IDC. "IDC Finds Internet Advertising Keeps Growing Fast Despite Economic Difficulties." *IDC.* May 30, 2008. http://www.idc.com/getdoc.jsp?containerId=prUS21260308 (accessed June 16, 2008).

20. Invesp Consulting. "The State of Online Advertising." *Invesp Consulting.* 2008. http://www.invesp.com/docs/invesp-state-of-online-advertising.pdf (accessed June 16, 2008).

21. Southern Economic Development Council 2008 Summer Session. July 10, 2008. Kissimmee, Florida.

22. Klein, Eva. "Your Regional Knowledge Economy Strategy: Is it Succeeding?" *Economic Development America*, Spring 2007.

23. Sweeney, Mark, personal interview. July 16, 2008.

24. Although the survey did not identify where the site location advisors were locating manufacturing projects, the responses showed that 60% provide site location services in multiple countries.

25. Foote, Deane, personal interview. July 23, 2008.

26. Schjeldahl, Don, personal interview. July 16, 2008.

27. Donovan, Dennis, personal interview. July 16, 2008.

28. Monger, Tim, personal interview. July 16, 2008.

29. Ubalde, Anatalio and Simundza, Eric. *Site Selection in an Information Era*, 2008. A survey of site selection consultants and corporate real estate professionals was conducted at the same time as the survey of economic developers. The respondents of the site selection survey included many of the most notable site location consulting firms and corporations. A full list of the respondents is included in Appendix B, Table B-1.

30. These differences between EDCs and government are significant at the 95% confidence level. The difference between Chambers of Commerce, EDCs, and government were all significant at the 95% confidence level also; however, for this type of statistical comparison it is preferable to have populations of equal size, which is not the

case for this survey sample because there were fewer Chambers that responded.

31. The creative class, a phrase coined by professor and author Richard Florida and made famous in his book *The Rise of the Creative Class* published in 2003, refers to a population of professionals that work in the sort of creative, post-industrial fields most typically located in urban centers. Whereas a community's economic success is typically thought to be tied to the creation of jobs, a growing number of those involved in economic development believe that communities must shift their focus from creating jobs to providing places where the creative class will want to live. Research in the community preferences of young professionals has been pioneered by Rebecca Ryan in her book *Live First, Work Second*, published in 2007.

32. The survey does not indicate the motivation for why economic development organizations are targeting these industries, but they are the same industries typically associated as those desirable by the creative class and young professionals.

33. These differences by population size are significant at the 95% confidence level.

34. Ryan, Rebecca, personal interview. June 17, 2008.

35. This difference by urbanity is significant at the 95% confidence level.

36. Boundaries were drawn based on states' membership in major regional economic development associations: members of the Northeastern Economic Developers Association (NEDA) made up the Northeast, members of the Southern Economic Development Council (SEDC) made up the South, members of the Mid-America Economic Development Council (MAEDC) made up the Midwest, and the remaining states were allocated to the West. Maryland, a member of both SEDC and NEDA, was grouped in the Northeast.

37. These regional differences are significant at the 95% confidence level, except the difference in website budgeting, which is significant

at the 90% confidence level.

38. The majority of respondents to the survey hold high-level positions. 89% are executives or managers in their organization. It is not surprising then that 75% of the respondents were also 40 years of age or older, including 41% who were at least 50 years old. Perhaps due to the smaller sample size of the younger economic developers, as well as the hesitancy for many respondents to divulge their age, there is no statistical significance of the variations of responses by age. However, the raw numbers do show variation.

39. Pew Research Center. "Demographics of Internet Users." February 15, 2008. http://www.pewinternet.org/trends/User_Demo_2.15.08.htm (accessed June 30, 2008).

40. Ryan, Rebecca. *Live First, Work Second.* Next Generation Consulting. 2007. There is also a dramatic difference in how people consume media based on age. It was recently found that for American adults (ages 12 and up), television accounted for two thirds of hours spent watching media, while one third was spent with newer media types: the Internet, DVDs, game consoles, and mobile devices. For 12-to-24-year-olds, these ratios were reversed. For more information, read: Coplan, Jill Hamburg. "Sleep, Work, Watch." *The Business Week*, June 30, 2008.

41. International Economic Development Council Marketing and Attraction Training Course. Atlanta, Georgia. Feb. 29, 2008.

42. Software as a service (SaaS) is a service model where users are granted access to applications from a central service provider. SaaS frees users from the burdens of software maintenance, ongoing operation, and support. In addition, on-demand pricing for SaaS may reduce up-front costs for users. An example of a company that has been a leader in SaaS is Salesforce.com. For more information on SaaS, read: Software & Information Industry Association. "Software as a Service: Strategic Backgrounder." SIIA. 2000. http://www.siia.net/estore/ssb-01.pdf (accessed May 28, 2008).

43. It is very important to note that although a comparison between economic developers and corporate real estate site selectors is provided, the reader of this book should not infer that one of these groups is more correct than the other or that one should follow the tendencies of the other. Instead, it is simply a comparison for use by economic developers that are specifically targeting corporate real estate professionals and site selection consultants.

44. Ubalde, Anatalio and Eric Simundza. *Site Selection in an Information Era*, 2008.

45. Donovan, Dennis, personal interview. July 16, 2008.

46. Ady, Robert "The Internet has Changed the Dynamics of Site Selection: What it Means for Your Business." *Forbes*. May 2006.

47. Donovan, Dennis, personal interview. July 16, 2008.

48. Ady, Robert "The Internet has Changed the Dynamics of Site Selection: What it Means for Your Business." *Forbes*. May 2006.

49. O'Reilly, Tim. "What Is Web 2.0." *O'Reilly Media*. September 30, 2005. http://www.oreillynet.com/pub/a/oreilly/tim/news/2005/09/30/what-is-web-20.html (accessed May 28, 2008).

50. Buchanan, Leigh, Max Chafkin, and Ryan McCarthy. "The New Basics of Marketing." *Inc.*, February 2008: 75-81.

51. The question for benchmarking marketing asked organizations to rank their top five criteria, allowing for analysis on how organizations weighted their choices. Due to the large number of answer choices for the separate question for benchmarking overall success, organizations were asked only to select their top five criteria. Table C-9 in the Appendix displays the criteria for benchmarking marketing in a similar format to the table for benchmarking overall success.

52. Southern Economic Development Council. "SEDC's 2007 Annual Conference." *SEDC News*, Fall 2007.

53. Forman, Eric. "Slowing Economy Drives Information Demand." *Realcomm Advisory*, June 26, 2008.

54. Rubin, Herbert. "Shoot Anything that Flies; Claim Anything that Falls: Conversations with Economic Development Practitioners." *Economic Development Quarterly* 2, no. 3 (August 1988): 236-251.